RETIREMENT PLANNING REVOLUTIONIZED

UNLOCK SECRETS TO NEVER OUTLIVE YOUR SAVINGS, CONFIDENTLY NAVIGATE FINANCIAL INVESTMENTS, MINIMIZE RISK, AND SECURE YOUR FUTURE

NICK ALOISIO

TABLE OF CONTENTS

INTRODUCTION

In 2008, I stood at a crossroads. I had just received a modest inheritance from my grandfather's lifelong investments. With it, I opened a Roth IRA. My grandfather was a disciplined investor who navigated the market's ups and downs with steady resolve. His example taught me invaluable lessons about growth and resilience. Yet, as I took my first steps into retirement planning, I realized something unsettling. The traditional savings methods seemed insufficient for the secure future I envisioned.

Fast-forward to 2021, a pivotal year in my financial journey. I discovered Bitcoin, a digital asset that promised a new way to think about investments. This discovery reshaped my retirement strategy, blending the time-tested principles I learned from my grandfather's example with the innovative potential of modern financial tools. This book is a culmination of that journey, crafted to empower you.

The core purpose of this book is to guide you toward a secure retirement. We will blend traditional and modern investment strategies, focusing on long-term financial security. Our goal is to ensure you do not outlive your savings, even amidst economic challenges. We live in uncertain times, where inflation and market volatility create widespread anxiety about the future. Rest assured, you are not alone in these concerns. Many worry about outliving their savings and the complexities of financial planning. This book offers practical solutions and personalized guidance to help you navigate these challenges.

Throughout the book, we will explore key concepts and themes. You will find detailed discussions on Roth IRAs and 401(k)s, those stalwarts of retirement planning. Alongside them, we will delve into modern options such as Bitcoin. By understanding how these tools can work together, you can enhance your retirement strategies and address the complexities of today's financial landscape.

What makes this book unique is its approach to integrating digital assets. We will explore the idea of Bitcoin as 'digital real estate.' Think of it as an appreciating, long-term store of value. This fresh perspective offers new ways to accumulate assets and preserve wealth.

The book is structured to guide you step-by-step. We will begin with foundational concepts, helping you understand the basics of retirement planning. From there, we will move to more advanced strategies, blending traditional tools with modern innovations. Each section builds on the last, providing a roadmap to secure retirement.

As you read this book, you can expect to gain practical tools and insights. We will explore real-life case studies and delve into both traditional and modern investment strategies. I hope you will feel confident applying these teachings to your financial journey, along with your research and input from a trusted financial advisor.

I invite you to explore this path of financial empowerment with me. Together, we will embrace both established and innovative methods to secure a fulfilling retirement. Welcome to a journey that blends the wisdom of the past with the promise of the future.

1

LAYING THE FOUNDATION FOR A SECURE RETIREMENT

When I started seriously thinking about retirement, I met with a financial advisor who outlined the stock market's history, emphasizing its steady growth over time and encouraging me to ignore the ups and downs. I questioned this approach after the 2008 crisis, when my employer stopped matching 401(k) contributions. I did the math on my Roth IRA and 401 (k), only to realize that I'd have barely more than a year's salary set aside by retirement age.

I knew I needed something different. In 2021, I discovered Bitcoin, which sparked a hope that traditional investments never had. I poured myself into learning everything I could about it, moving my Roth IRA into a Bitcoin IRA and even taking a loan from my 401(k) to buy more. The deeper I went, the more I believed that adding Bitcoin to my portfolio could transform my struggling retirement strategy into one poised for success.

It was then that I understood the necessity of a comprehensive approach to retirement planning. This approach navigates the complexities of traditional investments and embraces modern innovations. This chapter is dedicated to establishing that foundation and addressing the economic trends and challenges that shape our retirement landscape.

1.1 THE RETIREMENT PLANNING LANDSCAPE: CURRENT TRENDS AND CHALLENGES

As we examine the intricacies of retirement planning, it is crucial to understand the economic forces that influence our savings and investments. Inflation, a persistent rise in prices, poses a silent threat to retirement funds by eroding purchasing power over time. This financial phenomenon reduces the value of money, meaning that the dollars you save today will buy less in the future. According to Investopedia, while Social Security benefits attempt to adjust for inflation, these adjustments often fall short, leaving retirees with diminished purchasing power. As costs for essential goods and services climb, retirees must navigate this landscape by strategically investing in assets that keep pace with inflation, such as inflation-protected bonds or diversified income streams.

Interest rates, another critical factor, have been fluctuating, influencing everything from savings account yields to the performance of bonds. Lower interest rates can lead to lower savings returns, requiring retirees to seek alternative investment vehicles to maintain their income. This volatility calls for a careful balance in asset allocation, ensuring portfolios remain resilient against market shifts. Additionally, stagnant wages present a challenge for those still in the workforce, as the value of their earnings may not align with inflation, further complicating long-term savings efforts. Coupled with increasing longevity, which extends the period over which savings must last, these economic trends demand a proactive and adaptive retirement strategy.

Pre-retirees today face a myriad of challenges, chief among them being the rising costs of healthcare and long-term care. With healthcare expenses projected to continue upward, it is essential to incorporate these costs into retirement plans. Yet, many individuals find themselves unprepared, as a significant gap exists between expected and actual retirement savings. This gap often stems from insufficient financial literacy and early planning. As reported by Investopedia, retirees can mitigate some of these challenges by making informed decisions about housing, which can significantly impact financial stability. Downsizing or renting can reduce housing costs, freeing up resources for other needs.

Demographic shifts further complicate the retirement landscape. An aging population, particularly the wave of baby boomers entering retirement, affects individual planning and broader economic and policy considerations. Increased life expectancy means individuals must plan for longer retirement periods, often well beyond previous generations. This demographic shift places pressure on retirement systems and requires innovative solutions to ensure that savings are sufficient to support extended lifespans. As the population ages, the demand for retirement-related services and products grows, highlighting the importance of adapting strategies to meet these evolving needs.

In this era of rapid technological advancement, digital tools and platforms are reshaping how we approach retirement planning. Modern financial technology (FinTech) offers new opportunities to manage investments and optimize savings. Online financial planning tools provide accessible and user-friendly platforms for tracking expenses, setting goals, and modeling various retirement scenarios. As discussed in the Pension Research Council publication, Robo-advisors utilize complex algorithms to offer personalized investment advice, making sophisticated financial planning accessible to a broader audience. These innovations empower individuals to take control of their financial futures by providing real-time insights and automated solutions. As technology evolves, it introduces opportunities and challenges, necessitating a willingness to adapt and embrace new retirement planning methods.

1.2 ALIGNING RETIREMENT GOALS WITH PERSONAL VALUES AND LIFE ASPIRATIONS

The road to a fulfilling retirement begins with aligning financial plans with what truly matters to you. Value-driven financial planning is not just a strategy; it's a holistic approach to ensure your financial decisions reflect your personal values and aspirations. At its core, this method transforms retirement from a mere financial milestone into a deeply personal experience. By identifying core personal values, you create a blueprint for your financial future that resonates with who you are. This alignment guides investment choices and informs decisions about lifestyle preferences and how they fit into long-term financial goals. Whether it's prioritizing family, health, or personal enrichment, understanding what you value most allows you to craft a retirement strategy that is not only practical but also deeply satisfying.

The next step involves setting meaningful retirement goals tailored to these values. This process requires introspection and clarity. A practical tool to aid this is developing a retirement vision board. This visual representation captures your aspirations, illustrating what a successful retirement looks like for you. You turn abstract desires into actionable plans by prioritizing goals based on personal values. Consider a couple nearing retirement who values travel. By allocating resources specifically for travel experiences, they ensure that their financial strategy supports this passion, making retirement a phase of life and a continuation of their adventurous spirit. This approach transforms retirement planning into an engaging journey of self-discovery and personal growth.

Personalized retirement plans offer significant benefits by tailoring strategies to individual circumstances. This customization enhances satisfaction and financial security, providing a roadmap that adapts to life's unique twists and turns. For instance, consider a single parent who prioritizes their child's education. Their retirement plan might include specific savings goals for tuition, ensuring their financial stability while supporting their child's future. Such plans provide a structured yet flexible framework, allowing individuals to adapt to changes while remaining aligned with their core values. By embracing this personalized approach, individuals can create a retirement experience that is both rewarding and resilient.

Aligning values with financial decisions also has a profound psychological impact. This alignment reduces stress and boosts confidence as financial choices become a natural extension of one's values. When your financial path aligns with your values, the mental burden of decision-making lessens. You gain peace of mind knowing your financial future supports what truly matters to you. This link between financial decisions and mental well-being cannot be overstated. It transforms retirement planning from a source of anxiety into a process of empowerment. Strategies for maintaining this alignment during financial changes include regular reflection and open communication with trusted advisors, ensuring that financial decisions continue to reflect personal values.

Understanding this connection can also enhance your financial literacy and decision-making skills. One effective method for maintaining alignment is through regular financial reviews.

Individuals can ensure that their financial strategies remain relevant by setting aside time to reassess priorities and goals. This proactive approach allows for adjustments in response to life changes, such as shifts in family dynamics or unexpected expenses. Another strategy is to engage in open dialogue with financial advisors who understand your values and can provide guidance tailored to your unique needs. This collaborative approach fosters a sense of partnership and trust, empowering you to confidently make informed decisions.

Some may choose to align their financial decisions with personal values by supporting industries that promote sustainability, innovation, and well-being while avoiding those that may not align with their principles. Bitcoin, for example, offers a unique option with its decentralized, transparent system, which operates on a game theory that encourages cooperation over conflict, potentially fostering a path toward global peace and a healthier society.

Ultimately, aligning retirement goals with personal values is an evolving dynamic process. It requires a willingness to adapt and a commitment to staying true to what matters most. By embracing this value-driven approach, you lay the groundwork for a retirement that is financially secure and rich in personal fulfillment. As you embark on this path, remember that your values are the compass guiding your financial decisions. They illuminate the way forward, ensuring that your retirement is a reflection of your true self.

1.3 THE IMPORTANCE OF EARLY AND STRATEGIC PLANNING FOR LONG-TERM SECURITY

Early planning is a cornerstone of a secure financial future. Those who begin retirement planning early are more likely to revel in the fruits of their labor later in life. An early start allows you the luxury of compound interest and provides the flexibility to adjust your strategy over time. Compound interest, which is sometimes referred to as the eighth wonder of the world, helps your investments grow exponentially. By reinvesting the interest earned, your savings can accumulate significantly over decades. For instance, if you begin saving $3,000 annually at age 25, the power of compound interest can produce a considerable nest egg by retirement. In contrast, starting at 35 with the same annual contribution can lead to far less growth, illustrating the significant impact of time and compounding.

Strategic planning is just as vital. Creating a flexible financial roadmap that incorporates risk management strategies is crucial for long-term security. This roadmap should not be a rigid plan but a living document that evolves as circumstances change. Flexibility allows you to adapt to life's uncertainties, such as shifts in income, health, or family dynamics. By incorporating risk management strategies, you can safeguard your investments against market volatility. Diversifying your portfolio and balancing growth and security are critical components of a robust plan. The goal is to put together a retirement strategy that meets your financial needs and matches your personal values and aspirations.

Education and continuous learning play a pivotal role in successful retirement planning. The financial landscape is ever-changing, and staying informed is essential. Numerous resources are available for ongoing financial education, from online courses to workshops and seminars. By adopting a perspective of continuous learning, you can remain abreast of new financial tools and trends. Financial advisors can also be invaluable in providing guidance tailored to your unique situation. They can help you with complex investment decisions, assuring your approach aligns with your objectives. Engaging with a trusted advisor who understands your needs and values can significantly enhance your planning efforts.

Adaptability is another critical element of retirement planning. The ability to adjust your plans in response to life's unpredictability is what sets successful planners apart. For example, building contingency plans for economic downturns can provide a financial safety net. This might include setting aside emergency funds or adjusting your investment strategy to weather market fluctuations. Flexibility in adjusting asset allocations allows you to respond to changes in risk tolerance or financial goals. By regularly reviewing and rebalancing your portfolio, you can ensure that your strategy remains on track. The key is to stay proactive, revisit your plan periodically, and make adjustments as needed.

Incorporating these strategies into your retirement plan can lead to a more secure and fulfilling future. Starting early, planning strategically, staying informed, and remaining adaptable sets the stage for financial success. This approach safeguards your financial well-being and empowers you to pursue the retirement lifestyle you envision.

1.4 CRAFTING A UNIQUE RETIREMENT VISION: BEYOND FINANCIAL SECURITY

As we contemplate the golden years of retirement, it is important to look beyond the numbers and consider the life we want to lead. Financial security, while important, is just one piece of the puzzle. A truly fulfilling retirement encompasses all dimensions of life, marrying financial goals with personal fulfillment. Picture your daily routine not just from an economic standpoint but as a reflection of your deepest desires. It is about finding a balance between managing your finances and engaging in activities that bring joy and meaning. Whether it's spending time with friends and family, exploring new hobbies, or volunteering, these elements create a rich tapestry of adventures that define a satisfying retirement.

Exploring the non-financial aspects reveals the significance of social engagement, hobbies, and personal growth. Building a supportive social network is paramount. This network, composed of friends, family, and community, provides both emotional and practical support, enriching our lives in myriad ways. Opportunities for lifelong learning and volunteering offer avenues for personal growth and contribute to a sense of purpose. Engaging in activities that challenge the mind and nurture the spirit can be as rewarding as any financial achievement. For instance, joining a local book club or mentoring young professionals can foster connections and stimulate intellectual curiosity. These pursuits enhance our lives and create ripples of positive impact in the lives of others.

Crafting a comprehensive retirement vision involves clarity and intention. Begin by reflecting on what really matters to you. Vision workshops and reflection exercises can aid in articulating these aspirations. Consider crafting a retirement "bucket list" that captures your dreams and goals. This list acts as a guiding star, steering your decisions and providing motivation. It might include travel destinations, new skills to learn, or personal milestones to achieve. Revisiting and revising this list as your interests evolve ensures it remains a dynamic tool for shaping your retirement. By envisioning a future filled with purpose and passion, you lay the groundwork for a retirement that is not only secure but also deeply fulfilling.

Real-life examples offer valuable insights into crafting a unique retirement vision. Consider the story of a couple who redefined their retirement by combining travel with volunteer work. They spent part of each year volunteering in different countries, using their skills to contribute to local communities. This unconventional path allowed them to explore the world while making a meaningful impact. Another example is a retiree who transformed a lifelong passion for gardening into a community project, teaching sustainable practices and inspiring others. Such varied retirement lifestyles demonstrate that there is no one-size-fits-all approach. Drawing inspiration from these stories allows us to explore diverse possibilities and tailor our retirement to suit our unique preferences and circumstances.

In closing, envisioning retirement as a holistic experience invites us to think beyond the confines of financial planning. It encourages us to pursue a life rich with experiences, relationships, and personal growth. By aligning our financial strategies with our deepest values and aspirations, we can create a retirement that is financially secure and profoundly rewarding. As we embark on this process, let us embrace the possibilities and craft a future that reflects the best of who we are. With thoughtful planning and a clear vision, we can look forward to a retirement rich with joy, purpose, and fulfillment.

2

MASTERING THE BASICS: TRADITIONAL RETIREMENT TOOLS

In a world where financial security seems elusive, understanding the basics of retirement planning becomes not just a necessity but a form of empowerment. Picture yourself standing at the edge of a vast ocean, the horizon representing your future. You need a sturdy vessel built on sound financial principles to navigate this ocean. This chapter aims to supply you with the knowledge of traditional retirement tools that serve as the keel of that vessel, providing stability and direction. Here, we'll explore the intricacies of Roth IRAs, a cornerstone of retirement planning that offers tax advantages and flexibility, ensuring you can sail smoothly toward a secure future.

Roth IRAs stand out as one of the most powerful tools in your retirement arsenal. These accounts let you contribute after-tax dollars, which means the money you invest grows tax-free and, upon retirement, can be withdrawn without any tax penalties. This arrangement proves particularly beneficial for those expecting to be in a higher tax bracket during their retirement years, allowing them to maximize their savings potential. Unlike traditional IRAs, Roth IRAs do not require mandatory withdrawals, offering you more control over your retirement funds. Eligibility to contribute hinges on your Modified Adjusted Gross Income (MAGI), with limits set to ensure fair access. For instance, in 2023, individuals earning below $138,000 or couples below $218,000 can contribute the full amount, which is $6,500 for those under 50 and $7,500 for those aged 50 and up, according to Schwab's guidelines.

Strategic timing is crucial for maximizing the benefits of a Roth IRA. The annual contribution limits reset each year, making it imperative to plan your contributions to take full advantage of these limits. By employing strategies like dollar-cost averaging, where your contributions are spread evenly throughout the year, you can mitigate risk associated with market volatility and ensure consistent growth of your investments. This approach helps you manage market fluctuations and instills a disciplined saving habit that can yield substantial returns over time. Contribution deadlines typically align with the tax filing deadline, allowing you ample time to maximize your annual input.

Roth IRA conversions offer another strategic avenue for enhancing your retirement portfolio. This process involves transferring funds from traditional retirement accounts, such as a 401(k) or a traditional IRA, into a Roth IRA. Though this conversion requires you to pay taxes on the transferred amount in the year of conversion, the long-term benefits can be significant. By converting during years when your income is lower, you can minimize the tax impact and position yourself advantageously for future tax-free withdrawals. Calculating the tax implications requires careful planning, often necessitating the expertise of financial advisors to ensure maximum tax efficiency. It's a delicate balance of timing and foresight, aiming to optimize your retirement funds while minimizing tax liabilities.

Consider the story of Anne, a mid-career professional who used her Roth IRA strategically to secure her retirement. Anne anticipated that her tax bracket would increase in retirement due to her pension and other income sources. To counter this, she steadily contributed to her Roth IRA, taking advantage of the tax-free growth. Anne also performed a strategic conversion during a sabbatical year, ensuring the tax impact was minimized. This proactive approach allowed her to retire with peace of mind, knowing her withdrawals would not be burdened by taxes. Her story exemplifies how understanding and leveraging the nuances of Roth IRAs can lead to a robust retirement strategy.

Now, reflect on how these principles can be applied to your own financial journey. Consider the potential of integrating Roth IRAs into your retirement plan. Assess your current and future tax brackets, explore the timing of contributions, and weigh the benefits of potential conversions. By doing so, you can tailor a strategy that aligns with your financial goals, providing a pathway to a secure and fulfilling retirement.

2.1 NAVIGATING 401(K) OPTIONS: EMPLOYER PLANS AND BEYOND

When planning your retirement, a 401(k) remains one of the most powerful tools available. This employer-sponsored plan allows you to save for retirement with pre-tax income, which can significantly reduce your taxable income each year. The tax advantages are clear—your contributions grow tax-deferred until you withdraw them, ideally during retirement, when you may be in a lower tax bracket. Many employers sweeten the pot by offering matching contributions, a benefit that can substantially boost your savings. For example, suppose 50 cents per dollar for the first 6% of your salary is matched by your employer. In that case, that's a 50% return on your investment before it even enters the market. However, it's crucial to understand the vesting schedules attached to these matches. Vesting determines when you fully own your employer's contributions, and the timeline can range from immediate vesting to a graded schedule over several years. Additionally, while 401(k) plans offer tax advantages, they come with limitations like withdrawal penalties before age 59½, which can eat into your savings if you're not careful.

Selecting the right investment options within your 401(k) can feel overwhelming, given the array of choices typically available. One approach is to consider target-date funds, which adjust their asset allocation automatically based on your expected year of retirement. These funds offer a hands-off strategy, ideal for those who prefer simplicity. Alternatively, if you wish to tailor your investments, you can select individual assets. This requires an understanding of your risk tolerance and investment horizon. Assessing these factors helps ensure your portfolio aligns with your financial goals and comfort level. If you're younger, you might lean towards equities for growth, while those nearing retirement might prefer a conservative mix with more bonds. Regularly reviewing and adjusting your allocations as your circumstances or market conditions change is a prudent practice to maintain a balanced portfolio.

Maximizing employer contributions is a straightforward way to enhance your 401(k) savings. Always try to contribute enough to take full advantage of your employer's match. Consider the match as free money that can significantly augment your retirement nest egg over time. The impact of these contributions is profound, as they compound over years, potentially adding thousands to your retirement fund. If your financial situation allows, gradually increase your contribution rate, especially when you receive salary raises or bonuses. Many plans offer automatic escalation features, incrementally increasing your contribution rate each year. This strategy can help you maximize your savings without feeling the immediate pinch in your take-home pay.

A common pitfall in 401(k) management is making early withdrawals, which can lead to steep penalties and taxes, significantly eroding your savings. Understanding these penalties and resisting the desire to tap into your 401(k) prematurely is vital. Instead, consider other sources for emergency funds, such as a separate savings account. Another area for improvement is to review and adjust your investment allocations regularly. As markets fluctuate and personal circumstances change, it's essential to revisit your portfolio to ensure it remains aligned with your goals. Falling into the set-it-and-forget-it trap can result in a misaligned investment strategy that doesn't reflect your evolving risk tolerance or retirement timeline. By staying proactive and informed, you can avoid these common mistakes and keep your retirement plan on track.

2.2 UNDERSTANDING ANNUITIES: STABILITY IN INCOME STREAMS

Annuities occupy a unique space in the realm of retirement planning, serving as a bridge between immediate financial security and the long-term, stable income that many retirees seek. At their core, annuities are contracts between you and an insurance company, where you contribute a sum of money and, in return, receive a series of payments either immediately or in the future. These products come in several forms, each with distinct features and benefits. Fixed annuities provide a guaranteed payout and shield you from market volatility, offering a predictable income stream. They are akin to the comfort of a steady paycheck, ensuring you can meet your daily expenses without financial stress. Variable annuities, on the other hand, link your returns to the performance of underlying investments, offering the potential for higher gains but with increased risk. Indexed annuities add another layer by tying their returns to a specific market index, like the S&P 500, blending elements of both fixed and variable annuities. They offer a middle ground, providing the potential for growth while protecting against significant losses.

Incorporating annuities into your retirement plan requires careful consideration of their pros and cons. One of the most appealing aspects of annuities is their ability to provide guaranteed income. This feature can bring peace of mind in the unpredictable economic climate. It can be particularly valuable if you are concerned about outliving your savings, as annuities offer a lifetime income option. However, it's important to weigh this against the potential downsides. Annuities often include high fees and surrender charges, which can erode their overall value.

Additionally, the fixed nature of returns in some annuities can expose you to inflation risk, reducing your purchasing power over time. This is a critical consideration, as inflation can significantly impact your ability to maintain your standard of living throughout retirement. By understanding these dynamics, you can make informed decisions about whether annuities align with your financial goals and risk tolerance.

Selecting the right annuity product and provider is a critical step to ensure that your investment aligns with your retirement objectives. When evaluating annuity providers, focus on their financial strength and reputation, as this will directly impact their ability to meet their obligations. Look for providers with high ratings from independent agencies, which can give you confidence in their stability and reliability. It's also important to entirely comprehend the terms and conditions of any annuity contract. Pay attention to details such as payout options, fees, and any conditions or restrictions that may apply. Some contracts may offer additional features, such as long-term care riders or inflation protection, which can add value but may also increase costs. By carefully reviewing these elements, you can select an annuity that complements your broader financial strategy and provides the security you seek.

Consider the story of Roberto and Linda, a couple who successfully integrated annuities into their retirement plan. With a mix of fixed and indexed annuities, they secured a portion of their income, ensuring they could cover essential expenses without dipping into their other investments. This strategy provided them with financial stability, allowing them to enjoy retirement without worrying about market fluctuations. They balanced their annuities with other income sources, such as Social Security and a small pension, creating a diversified income stream that met their needs. Their experience highlights the importance of considering annuities as part of a broader retirement plan, using them strategically to address specific financial goals and mitigate risks.

In another instance, consider Jane, a retiree who opted for a variable annuity to take advantage of potential market gains. She was comfortable with the associated risks and used the annuity to complement her other more conservative investments. This approach allowed her to benefit from market upswings while maintaining a level of financial security. Jane's story illustrates how annuities can be tailored to fit individual risk profiles and financial aspirations, offering a flexible tool for income stability.

2.3 LIFE INSURANCE AS A RETIREMENT TOOL: PROTECTION AND INVESTMENT

Life insurance often conjures images of financial safety nets for loved ones. However, its role in retirement planning extends beyond mere protection. It offers both security and investment opportunities. At its core, life insurance ensures that your beneficiaries obtain financial support in the event of your passing. This death benefit can be critical in safeguarding your family's financial future and alleviating the economic burden during a challenging time. However, life insurance also harbors the potential for cash value accumulation, particularly in permanent policies, which can be leveraged to enhance your retirement strategy. As you contribute to these policies, part of your premium is deposited into a cash value account, growing over time. This growth is accessible through policy loans or withdrawals, providing you with a flexible financial resource.

When choosing, it's important to understand the differences between term and permanent life insurance. The more affordable option, term life insurance, offers coverage for a limited time. It is a straightforward option for those seeking temporary financial protection. However, it lacks the cash value component and can become costly if renewed later in life. Unlike term life insurance, permanent life insurance—such as whole life and universal life policies—offers lifelong protection and includes a cash value component. Although initially more expensive, these policies offer the potential for cash value growth. This can be an attractive feature for those looking to integrate life insurance into their retirement planning. The ability to borrow against the cash value or use it as supplemental income adds a layer of financial flexibility, though it requires careful management to avoid reducing the death benefit.

Leveraging life insurance effectively in retirement involves understanding its strategic uses. Consider the cash value in permanent policies as a supplemental income source. This can be especially helpful during market declines, as withdrawing from traditional investment accounts could result in losses. By tapping into the cash value, you can maintain your lifestyle without depleting other savings. However, it is essential to be mindful of the tax implications. While loans against the cash value are typically tax-free, withdrawals that exceed the premiums paid may incur taxes. Grasping these details can guide you in making informed choices about when and how to utilize your policy's cash value.

Take, for example, the story of the Thompsons, a family who strategically used life insurance as part of their retirement plan. They opted for a whole life policy early, allowing the cash value to grow over decades. When they retired, they used the accumulated cash value to supplement their income, enabling them to travel and enjoy their hobbies without dipping into their primary savings. The death benefit remained intact, ensuring their children were financially secure. Their experience underscores the importance of integrating life insurance thoughtfully into retirement planning, aligning it with broader financial goals.

Another example is Sarah, an entrepreneur who used her life insurance policy creatively. Anticipating potential short-term cash flow needs, she took a policy loan to invest in her business without touching her retirement accounts. This decision allowed her business to thrive, eventually increasing her overall wealth. Sarah's approach highlights how life insurance can serve as a versatile financial tool, providing liquidity when needed.

Incorporating life insurance into your retirement strategy requires a comprehensive view of your financial landscape. It is about more than just protecting your legacy; it's about enhancing your financial flexibility and security. When evaluating your options, consider the costs and benefits while aligning them with your long-term goals. Recognizing how life insurance fits into your retirement strategy can offer peace of mind and financial stability. As you reflect on these strategies, consider how they might complement your existing plans and enhance your retirement outlook.

This chapter has explored the multifaceted role of life insurance in retirement planning, adding another layer to your financial toolkit. The next chapter will examine some innovative investment strategies that can further secure your financial future.

3

INNOVATIVE INVESTMENT STRATEGIES FOR THE MODERN RETIREE

"Everybody thinks Bitcoin is risky because it's volatile. It's volatile because it's not risky. It's the lowest-risk thing you can own in the world because it's the thing that has the most risk stripped away. The reason it's volatile is that it's the most desirable, most accessible thing, which means that everybody else is expressing their sentiment and their emotions every minute of the day, everywhere in the world, however they wish to."

— MICHAEL SAYLOR

On a crisp autumn evening in 2008, the world was on the brink of financial chaos. The collapse of Lehman Brothers marked a pivotal moment, thrusting economies into turmoil and revealing the vulnerabilities of traditional banking systems. This crisis wasn't just a financial event but a catalyst that spurred innovation. In the shadows of this upheaval, a revolutionary idea was quietly taking shape. An enigmatic figure named Satoshi Nakamoto, whose true identity remains cloaked in mystery, released a white paper that introduced Bitcoin, a digital currency designed to operate outside the control of centralized financial institutions. This moment marked the dawn of a new era in finance, one that promised to redefine the very concept of money.

The creation of Bitcoin was not a mere technological feat but a response to the systemic failures that had become painfully evident. The financial crisis of 2008 revealed the global banking system's vulnerabilities, characterized by risky financial products, inadequate regulation, and a lack of transparency. In this context, Satoshi's vision introduced a decentralized solution built on blockchain technology. This digital ledger securely and transparently records transactions across a network of computers. The first actual Bitcoin transaction occurred on May 22, 2010, when a programmer named Laszlo Hanyecz purchased two pizzas for 10,000 bitcoins, a moment now celebrated as Bitcoin Pizza Day. This transaction, though modest at the time, marked Bitcoin's transformation from an abstract idea to a practical currency.

Bitcoin's rise has been meteoric, fueled by its distinctive characteristics aligning with sound money principles. Sound money, in its essence, maintains its value over time and is resistant to manipulation. Bitcoin's fixed supply of 21 million units ensures scarcity, akin to precious metals like gold. The need for intermediaries is removed due to its decentralized nature, reducing the chance of corruption and inflationary pressures often associated with traditional fiat currencies. Moreover, Bitcoin's global accessibility allows for seamless transactions across borders, challenging the constraints of conventional financial systems. These properties make Bitcoin an appealing option for those seeking an alternative form of wealth preservation.

As the cryptocurrency landscape evolved, it expanded beyond Bitcoin, giving rise to various altcoins. These other cryptocurrencies, such as Ethereum and Solana, offer distinct features and use cases. Ethereum, for example, introduced the notion of smart contracts, self-executing contracts with the agreement terms directly written into its code. This innovation cleared the way for decentralized applications, creating a vibrant ecosystem where developers can build solutions without centralized oversight. Solana focuses on scalability and speed, enabling lower costs and faster processing through its unique Proof of History mechanism, offering speedier transaction speeds compared to Bitcoin. While these altcoins present exciting opportunities, they also come with increased volatility and risk, requiring careful consideration by investors.

The performance of altcoins relative to Bitcoin varies significantly over time. Bitcoin is the most well-known and firmly established cryptocurrency, often serving as a benchmark for the market. Its price movements can influence the broader crypto market. However, altcoins can experience more dramatic fluctuations due to their smaller market capitalizations and unique value propositions. For instance, Ethereum's value has significantly increased, driven by the expanding use of decentralized finance (DeFi) applications. At the same time, Solana's price has been impacted by regulatory scrutiny. These are crucial dynamics for investors looking to integrate cryptocurrencies into their portfolios, as each asset carries its own set of risks and rewards.

Reflection Exercise: Assessing Your Cryptocurrency Comfort Level

Before diving into cryptocurrency investments, take a moment to reflect on your risk tolerance and investment goals. Consider the following questions:

1. How comfortable are you with market volatility and the potential for significant price swings?
2. What percentage of your overall investment portfolio are you willing to allocate to cryptocurrencies?
3. Are you interested in diversifying within the cryptocurrency market by investing in alt-coins, or do you prefer to focus solely on Bitcoin?

Reflecting on these questions can help you determine the role of cryptocurrencies in your retirement strategy and guide your investment decisions moving forward.

3.1 BITCOIN AS DIGITAL REAL ESTATE: A NEW ASSET CLASS

Imagine owning a chunk of prime real estate, not in bustling New York City, but in the digital realm. This is the transformative potential that Bitcoin offers as an investment opportunity. It has been likened to digital real estate, a concept that captures its role as a store of value and a means to build long-term wealth. Just as New York property appreciates over time due to its desirability and limited availability, Bitcoin possesses similar traits. Its fixed supply of 21 million units ensures scarcity, driving its value appreciation as demand increases. This scarcity, coupled with universal desirability, makes Bitcoin a compelling asset in an era where traditional investments often fail to keep pace with inflation. As a digital asset, Bitcoin offers several advantages over physical real estate. It is portable, allowing you to move your investment across borders without the complexities of property transactions. Its fungibility and divisibility mean you can buy or sell fractions of Bitcoin, providing flexibility that real estate lacks. Moreover, Bitcoin requires no maintenance, freeing you from the burdens of property upkeep or tenant management. Its scalability and accessibility appeal to a broad range of investors, from seasoned financiers to tech-savvy millennials.

Investing in Bitcoin presents both remarkable opportunities and notable risks. On the one hand, it offers the potential for high returns, especially in a low-interest environment where traditional savings vehicles yield minimal gains. Bitcoin's historical performance has demonstrated significant appreciation, drawing attention from both individual investors and institutional players. However, with high potential returns come high volatility. Bitcoin's price can fluctuate dramatically, influenced by market sentiment, regulatory developments, and technological advancements. This volatility requires a robust risk management strategy to avoid substantial losses.

Additionally, regulatory uncertainties pose challenges as governments struggle to classify and regulate cryptocurrencies. Security is another critical concern; safeguarding your Bitcoin through secure storage solutions is paramount to prevent theft or loss. These factors necessitate careful consideration and a clear investment strategy.

Incorporating Bitcoin into your retirement portfolio can be strategic, provided you approach it with caution and foresight. A small allocation to Bitcoin can act as a hedge against inflation, preserving your purchasing power over time. To mitigate Bitcoin's inherent volatility, consider employing a dollar-cost averaging strategy. This involves buying a set amount at routine intervals, reducing the impact of market instabilities, and lowering the average cost of acquisition over time. Such an approach allows you to benefit from Bitcoin's potential upside while managing risk. Combining traditional investments with Bitcoin can strengthen your portfolio's resilience and growth potential, providing a balanced strategy for retirement planning.

Consider the story of early adopters who recognized Bitcoin's potential and integrated it into their investment strategies. Take, for example, the case of a tech entrepreneur who allocated a portion of their portfolio to Bitcoin in its nascent stages. Over time, this decision paid off, significantly enhancing their wealth and providing financial freedom. However, not all stories are success stories. Some investors succumbed to market hype, investing without a clear strategy and suffering losses during market downturns. These lessons underscore the importance of thorough research, planning, and risk management when investing in Bitcoin.

A notable example of a company leveraging Bitcoin is MicroStrategy, led by CEO Michael Saylor. In 2021, MicroStrategy made headlines by adding Bitcoin to its balance sheet, viewing it as a superior store of value compared to cash. This decision was driven by a belief in Bitcoin's potential to outperform traditional assets in the long term. MicroStrategy's stock price has outpaced Bitcoin itself, earning it the nickname "Infinite Money Glitch" for its innovative treasury strategy. This audacious move underscores the transformative possibility of Bitcoin in corporate finance, influencing other companies to consider similar strategies. MicroStrategy's plan to purchase additional Bitcoin worth $42 billion in the coming years is expected to impact the Bitcoin supply significantly. For individual investors, MicroStrategy's stock (MSTR) offers a chance to gain Bitcoin exposure through a publicly traded company, providing an alternative avenue for diversifying one's portfolio.

Annualized Asset Performance Chart Over Four Years

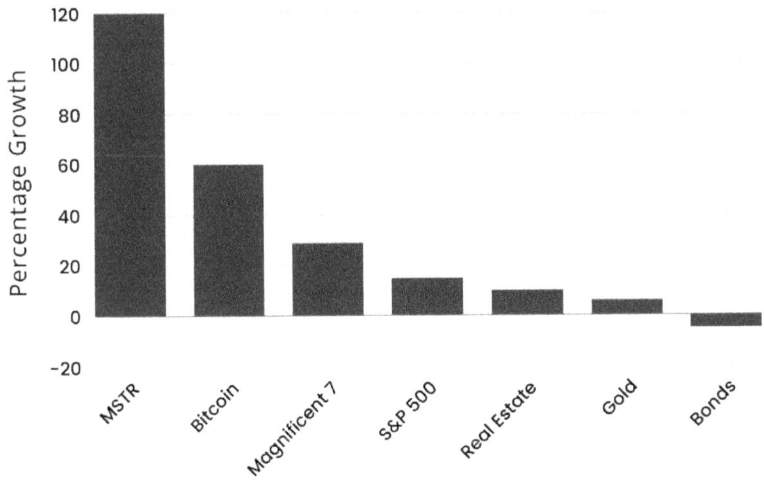

Performance since August 10, 2020, when MicroStrategy adopted its Bitcoin strategy.

Source: FactSet as of November 12, 2024

3.2 DIVERSIFICATION BEYOND BORDERS: INTERNATIONAL INVESTMENTS

When considering the resilience of a retirement portfolio, the concept of international diversification becomes increasingly significant. Expanding investments beyond domestic borders allows you to tap into a wealth of opportunities that enhance growth potential while mitigating risks inherent to any single market. Global investments offer access to emerging markets often marked by rapid economic development and innovation. Countries like Brazil, India, and China present dynamic environments where industries are evolving, potentially leading to higher returns. These markets might carry more volatility, yet they also offer a chance to be part of substantial growth trajectories. By including such assets, you spread risk across various economic landscapes, reducing the impact of adverse events in any single location.

To effectively navigate international markets, a strategic approach is vital. One practical method is investing in international mutual funds and exchange-traded funds (ETFs). These financial instruments pool resources to invest in a diverse range of global assets, offering broad exposure while minimizing individual security risks. When selecting these funds, it's crucial to evaluate geopolitical risks and currency fluctuations, as these factors can significantly influence investment outcomes. Comprehending economic indicators such as GDP growth, inflation rates, and political stability in foreign markets provides a more precise portrait of potential risks and rewards. Recognizing these elements guides informed decision-making, helping you pick assets that align with your risk tolerance and financial goals.

Foreign currencies play a pivotal role in diversification by providing a hedge against domestic currency risk. By investing in currency ETFs or mutual funds, you gain exposure to foreign currencies, which can balance instabilities in the domestic currency's value against your portfolio. Engaging with the foreign exchange (Forex) market, the largest global financial market, offers opportunities to capitalize on currency movements. Although Forex trading can be complex and requires a nuanced understanding of market dynamics, it can be a useful instrument for investors aiming to diversify their holdings. This approach diversifies financial assets and protects purchasing power, ensuring your retirement funds retain value despite economic shifts.

Consider the stories of retirees who have successfully diversified their portfolios internationally. One example is a couple who allocated a portion of their retirement savings to emerging market ETFs. This decision allowed them to benefit from the economic growth and rapid industrialization in regions like Southeast Asia. Over time, their diversified portfolio provided greater returns than a purely domestic focus. Another retiree invested in developed markets, finding stability in countries with established economies like Germany and Japan. This strategy provided consistent returns, balancing the higher volatility of emerging markets. These examples highlight the importance of a balanced approach, combining investments in both emerging and developed markets to optimize growth potential while managing risk.

In conclusion, embracing international diversification is not just about seeking higher returns but also about creating a robust, resilient portfolio that can withstand the uncertainties of a globalized economy. By incorporating international assets and currencies, you enhance the stability of your retirement savings, positioning yourself to navigate the financial world's complexities with security and confidence.

3.3 LEVERAGING TECHNOLOGY: THE ROLE OF ROBO-ADVISORS

In today's digital age, technology has remade the landscape of investment management, making it more accessible and efficient. Robo-advisors, automated platforms that manage portfolios using algorithms, have become a popular investment option for those seeking simplicity and cost-effectiveness. These platforms offer a streamlined approach to managing investments by providing automated rebalancing, which helps coordinate your portfolio with your resilience to risk and retirement objectives. Additionally, many robo-advisors incorporate tax-loss harvesting, a strategy that helps minimize taxes on investment gains by offsetting them with losses. This attribute especially helps investors who aim to maximize their after-tax returns while maintaining a balanced portfolio.

The appeal of robo-advisors lies in their cost advantage over traditional financial advisors. With lower fees, often starting around 0.25% of the assets under management, robo-advisors provide an affordable alternative for those who do not need personalized financial planning. However, this affordability comes with certain limitations. While robo-advisors excel in portfolio management, they may not offer the tailored advice that a human advisor can provide. This absence of personalization can be a disadvantage for retirees with complex financial situations or those who desire a more nuanced investment strategy. Despite these limitations, the convenience and efficiency of robo-advisors make them an attractive option for many.

Choosing the right robo-advisor involves careful consideration of your individual financial goals. Key evaluation features include the platform's fee structure, investment options, and additional services. Some robo-advisors provide access to human advisors for a higher fee, which can be a valuable resource for more complex financial planning needs. Integrating a robo-advisor into your existing financial strategy requires an understanding of how it complements your overall investment plan. Ensuring that your selected platform aligns with your risk tolerance, time horizon, and retirement goals is crucial. Doing so lets you leverage technology to enhance your investment strategy while maintaining control over your financial future.

As cryptocurrency gains popularity, a new breed of robo-advisors specializing in digital assets has emerged. Crypto robo-advisors cater to investors looking to incorporate cryptocurrencies into their portfolios. Unlike traditional robo-advisors, which focus on stocks and bonds, crypto robo-advisors provide insights and management tailored to the volatile nature of digital currencies. Some users find value in using both types of advisors to gain a complete picture of their investments, as traditional and digital assets require different strategies and risk assessments. Feedback from users suggests that while crypto robo-advisors offer specialized expertise, they are best used with broader financial tools to achieve a well-rounded investment approach.

Consider the story of John, a retiree who turned to robo-advisors to simplify his investment management. With a modest portfolio, John appreciated the lower fees and automated features that kept his investments aligned with his goals. Over time, he noticed improved portfolio performance and significant cost savings compared to his previous arrangements with a traditional advisor. John's experience highlights the potential benefits of incorporating technology into retirement planning, providing ease of use and satisfaction with minimal effort. For those like John, robo-advisors offer a practical solution to managing investments in a straightforward and efficient manner.

As we conclude this chapter, it is clear that technology continues to reshape how we approach retirement planning. Robo-advisors exemplify the power of automation in creating cost-effective and efficient investment solutions. As you integrate these tools into your strategy, consider how they align with your broader financial goals and how they can enhance your journey toward a secure and fulfilling retirement.

4

TAX OPTIMIZATION IN RETIREMENT PLANNING

Imagine peering through a window of opportunity that unveils a path to financial freedom, where your retirement savings grow, and you are shielded from the grasp of taxes. This is the promise of tax optimization, a strategy that allows you to retain more of your hard-earned money. Understanding tax efficiency becomes crucial as you navigate the complexities of retirement planning. It's not merely about accumulating wealth, but also ensuring that your savings work for you in the most effective way. This chapter explores the art of Roth conversions. This powerful tool can transform your tax landscape and enhance your financial security in retirement.

The concept of Roth conversions involves moving funds from a traditional IRA, where contributions grow tax-deferred, to a Roth IRA, which offers tax-free growth and withdrawals. Traditional IRAs require tax payments upon withdrawal, potentially leading to a higher tax burden during retirement. In contrast, Roth IRAs allow you to take distributions tax-free, provided certain conditions are met, such as the five-year rule.

This difference in tax treatment makes Roth conversions appealing for individuals expecting a higher tax bracket during retirement. By strategically converting funds, you can prepay taxes now, lock in today's rates, and enjoy tax-free income when needed.

Timing is everything when it comes to executing Roth conversions. Choosing the optimal moment can significantly impact your tax liability. One effective strategy is to capitalize on lower-income years, such as periods of unemployment or early retirement, when your taxable income is reduced. This approach minimizes the tax impact of the conversion, allowing you to move funds at a lower cost. In addition, spreading conversions over several years can help avoid moving into a higher tax bracket. By converting smaller amounts annually, you can manage the tax implications more effectively, ensuring you only pay what is necessary.

To further mitigate conversion taxes, consider employing techniques that offset the taxable income generated by the conversion. One method is to use deductions or credits to lower your overall tax bill. For instance, significant medical expenses or charitable contributions can offset the income from the conversion, reducing your tax liability. Another approach is to conduct partial conversions over several years, gradually moving funds to maintain control over your tax bracket. This phased strategy allows you to balance the benefits of tax-free growth with manageable tax costs, creating a win-win scenario for your retirement planning.

Real-life examples illustrate the effectiveness of Roth conversion strategies in optimizing tax outcomes. Consider David, a retiree who successfully leveraged Roth conversions to enhance his financial situation. Due to a job transition, David faced a year of reduced income, prompting him to convert a portion of his traditional IRA to a Roth IRA. By doing so, he took advantage of his lower tax bracket, minimizing the conversion's impact on his finances. Over time, David continued to execute small conversions, spreading them across multiple years. This careful planning allowed him to build a substantial tax-free income stream, providing security and flexibility in retirement.

Another example is Lisa, who strategically used Roth conversions to secure her financial future. During a market downturn, Lisa converted a portion of her traditional IRA, capitalizing on the reduced account value to lower her tax liability. Lisa effectively minimized the cost by timing her conversion during a market dip, setting herself up for tax-free growth as markets recovered. Her story underscores the importance of market awareness and strategic timing in executing Roth conversions.

Reflection Exercise: Assessing Your Roth Conversion Potential

Consider your current financial situation and future tax expectations. Reflect on the following questions to determine if a Roth conversion aligns with your retirement goals:

1. Are you likely to be in a higher tax bracket during retirement than your current situation?
2. Do you anticipate any lower-income years that could provide a tax-efficient window for conversion?
3. How comfortable are you with paying taxes now in exchange for potential tax-free income in the future?

Reflecting on these questions can help you make informed decisions about integrating Roth conversions into your retirement strategy.

4.1 TAX-ADVANTAGED ACCOUNTS: BEYOND THE BASICS

When planning for retirement, it's crucial to look beyond the traditional 401(k)s and IRAs. Consider the potential of Health Savings Accounts (HSAs) and 529 plans. HSAs stand out as a versatile tool for covering immediate medical expenses and as a strategic component of retirement planning. These accounts offer triple tax savings: contributions are made pre-tax, earnings grow tax-free, and withdrawals for qualified medical expenses are tax-free. This trifecta makes HSAs a powerful vehicle for managing healthcare costs in retirement. By investing HSA funds, you can grow this nest egg, ensuring you have the resources to cover rising medical costs. Unlike Flexible Spending Accounts (FSAs), unused HSA funds roll over year after year, providing a growing safety net for future needs.

529 plans, designed for education savings, present another tax-advantaged opportunity. These accounts allow your contributions to grow tax-deferred, with tax-free withdrawals for qualified educational expenses. While primarily used for college tuition, 529 plans have evolved. Recent changes now permit their use for K-12 education and student loan repayments. This flexibility extends the utility of 529 plans, making them a strategic option for families planning ahead. By starting contributions early and benefiting from compound growth, you can significantly offset the burden of education costs. These accounts provide financial relief and align with broader life goals, ensuring your loved ones

have access to quality education without compromising your retirement security.

Maximizing the benefits of these accounts involves strategic planning. For HSAs, consider pre-tax payroll deductions to escape FICA taxes, further enhancing tax efficiency. If you're 55 or older, take advantage of catch-up contributions to bolster your savings. Investing in HSA funds, rather than holding them as cash, can accelerate growth, providing a more substantial buffer against future medical expenses. For 529 plans, consistent contributions are key. Automating deposits can help you stay disciplined, ensuring you steadily build a robust education fund. Additionally, consider state-sponsored plans that offer tax deductions or credits for contributions, amplifying your savings potential. By leveraging these strategies, you can fully exploit these accounts' tax advantages, aligning them with your long-term financial goals.

Integrating tax-advantaged accounts into a comprehensive retirement plan requires thoughtful coordination. Align your contributions with your retirement milestones, ensuring these accounts complement your broader financial strategy. Consider using HSA funds as a dedicated healthcare savings vehicle, preserving other retirement assets for nonmedical expenses. Similarly, position 529 plans as part of your legacy planning, potentially transferring unused funds to other beneficiaries or utilizing them for your lifelong learning pursuits. Coordinating distributions from these accounts can enhance tax efficiency, reducing your overall tax burden in retirement. Strategic withdrawals from HSAs, for example, can cover healthcare costs without impacting taxable income, freeing up other assets to grow tax-deferred.

Beyond the well-known options, explore lesser-known accounts like SEP IRAs, especially if you're a small business owner. SEP

IRAs offer significant contribution limits, allowing for substantial retirement savings with tax-deductible contributions. This can be particularly advantageous for entrepreneurs seeking flexible retirement solutions. Lifetime learning credits also provide valuable tax relief for those pursuing late-career education, offsetting costs and encouraging continuous personal development. By exploring these unique opportunities, you can tailor your retirement plan to your specific circumstances, maximizing the benefits of tax-advantaged accounts in alignment with your financial aspirations.

4.2 STRATEGIC WITHDRAWALS: MINIMIZING TAX IMPACT

When you think about retirement, it's crucial to consider how you will draw down your savings. The strategy you employ can significantly affect the taxes you pay and the longevity of your savings. A well-thought-out withdrawal plan can minimize taxes and extend the life of your nest egg. Timing your withdrawals strategically is an integral part of this process. Deciding to take money out of your retirement accounts can shift you into different tax brackets, impacting the taxes owed. Withdrawing a large sum in a single year can elevate your tax bracket, leading to a higher tax burden than necessary. To avoid these pitfalls, consider spreading out your withdrawals over several years. This approach lets you stay within a more favorable tax bracket, ensuring you pay less over time.

Determining the sequence of withdrawals from your various accounts is another crucial element. Generally, it's wise to prioritize drawing from taxable accounts first. These accounts do not have the tax-deferred or tax-free growth benefits of other retirement accounts, so using these funds first can minimize the impact on your overall tax bill. By doing this, you also allow your tax-advantaged accounts to continue growing. Delaying withdrawals from tax-deferred accounts, like traditional IRAs or 401(k)s, can be beneficial as these accounts grow without immediate tax implications. Moreover, by waiting until required minimum distributions (RMDs) kick in, you maximize the compound growth potential of these accounts while delaying tax payments.

Tax diversification plays a decisive role in withdrawal strategies. A mix of taxable, tax-deferred, and tax-free accounts gives you flexibility in managing taxes. Balancing withdrawals among these account types allows you to optimize your tax situation each year. For example, in a year with higher income, you might focus on withdrawing from a Roth IRA, which allows for tax-free withdrawals, thereby avoiding additional income taxes. Conversely, in a lower-income year, taking distributions from a traditional IRA or 401(k) might be more advantageous. Adjusting your strategy annually, based on your financial situation, can significantly impact your overall tax liabilities and the longevity of your savings.

Consider the story of Mark and Suzan, a retired couple who carefully planned their withdrawal strategy to manage taxes effectively. Mark and Suzan began their retirement by withdrawing from their taxable brokerage account, which provided them with the necessary income without triggering higher taxes. This allowed their tax-advantaged accounts to grow uninterrupted. As they aged and their income needs increased, they gradually shifted their withdrawals to their Roth IRA, taking advantage of tax-free income. By the time they were required to start taking RMDs from their traditional IRA, they had already minimized their taxable income through strategic planning. This careful balance of income sources helped them avoid tax spikes and maintain their desired lifestyle throughout retirement.

In another example, consider John, who applied a similar approach but with a focus on tax-efficient withdrawals. John prioritized his taxable accounts initially, allowing his Roth IRA to serve as a buffer during years with unexpected expenses. He avoided pushing into higher tax brackets by accessing tax-free funds when needed. This strategy reduced his tax burden and extended the life of his retirement savings. John's experience underscores the importance of having a flexible withdrawal plan that adapts to changing circumstances, ensuring financial stability and peace of mind in retirement.

Ultimately, the key to successful withdrawal strategies lies in understanding the intricacies of tax implications and having the foresight to plan accordingly.

4.3 LONG-TERM TAX PLANNING: A HOLISTIC APPROACH

As you consider your financial future, envision tax planning as a vital thread woven into the fabric of your retirement strategy. Long-term tax planning isn't just about today—it's about enhancing your financial security across the years. Proactive tax planning can significantly impact your overall wealth by anticipating changes in tax policy, which can otherwise disrupt even the most carefully laid plans. The tax landscape is ever-evolving, shaped by economic shifts, political changes, and social priorities. By staying informed and adaptable, you can position yourself to respond effectively to these changes, ensuring your financial plans remain robust and resilient.

Estate taxes and legacy considerations add another layer to your tax planning efforts. Estate taxes can substantially erode the wealth you intend to pass on to future generations. Planning for these taxes involves understanding your estate's value and employing strategies to minimize potential liabilities. This might include gifting strategies, establishing trusts, or leveraging charitable contributions. Integrating estate planning with tax strategies can help protect your legacy and ensure your wealth effectively supports your loved ones and preferred causes. This holistic approach to tax planning allows you to stitch together a comprehensive tapestry of financial security that endures beyond your lifetime.

Using appropriate tools and resources to manage tax planning is vital. Tax software and calculators offer valuable assistance, providing real-time insights into your tax situation. These tools can help you model various scenarios, giving you a clearer picture of potential outcomes. Engaging with professional tax advisors is equally important. These experts bring a wealth of knowledge and experience, helping you identify opportunities and avoid pitfalls. A tax advisor can provide tailored advice, ensuring your tax strategies align with your broader financial goals. Utilizing these resources equips you to make well-informed choices contributing to your financial stability and growth.

Integrating tax planning with your overall retirement strategy requires a coordinated effort. Your tax strategies should align seamlessly with your investment and withdrawal plans, creating a unified approach that maximizes your financial potential. This involves considering how different types of income and investments are taxed and adjusting your plans accordingly. Life changes like marriage, divorce, or childbirth can also impact your tax planning. By anticipating these changes and adapting your strategies, you ensure your tax planning remains agile and effective. This integration forms a cohesive framework supporting your financial objectives, allowing you to confidently navigate life's uncertainties.

Let's explore the story of Emma, who successfully integrated long-term tax planning into her retirement strategy. Emma recognized early on the importance of anticipating tax policy changes and sought the guidance of a seasoned tax advisor. Together, they developed a plan that included strategic gifting, trust establishment, and careful management of her investment accounts. Emma's proactive approach allowed her to minimize estate taxes and ensure her legacy. As tax laws evolved, Emma and her advisor regularly revisited her plan, making necessary adjustments. This adaptability preserved Emma's wealth, providing her family with a secure financial future.

Another example is Katsu, who faced a significant life change after retiring from a long career. Understanding the potential impact on his taxes, Katsu coordinated with his advisor to align his tax strategies with his new financial reality. By strategically managing his investments and withdrawals, Katsu was able to maintain a favorable tax position, reducing his overall tax burden. This careful planning extended the longevity of his savings, allowing him to enjoy a comfortable retirement without financial stress. Katsu's experience highlights the importance of integrating tax planning with broader financial goals, ensuring your strategies adapt to life's transitions.

In the tapestry of retirement planning, long-term tax planning is a critical thread that weaves together financial security, legacy protection, and adaptability. By embracing a holistic approach, you safeguard your wealth and create a roadmap that guides you through the complexities of tax policy and life changes. As you continue to explore your financial options, remember that proactive planning is your ally. It can bring clarity and confidence as you work toward an assured and fruitful retirement.

As we conclude this chapter, consider how tax efficiency can enhance your financial journey, setting the stage for the next chapter's exploration of risk management and economic security.

5

RISK MANAGEMENT AND FINANCIAL SECURITY

Imagine you're an artist, and your portfolio is your canvas. Each investment decision becomes a brushstroke, contributing to a masterpiece that reflects your financial future. The key to crafting a robust and lasting piece is balance. This balance—between risk and security—forms the backbone of a resilient portfolio, ensuring that your financial goals stand firm against the unpredictable tides of the market. Diversification across asset classes is a prudent strategy and a cornerstone of long-term economic stability.

A well-balanced portfolio is akin to a sturdy ship navigating turbulent seas. By allocating investments across stocks, bonds, and alternative assets, you create a diversified foundation that can weather market fluctuations. Stocks offer growth potential, while bonds deliver stability through their fixed-income returns. Alternative investments like real estate and commodities provide unique opportunities to enhance diversification. This mix mitigates risk by ensuring that no single asset class dominates your portfolio. Diversification acts as a buffer, spreading risk and smoothing out the volatility inherent in individual investments. According to Fidelity, a diversified portfolio can potentially improve returns by managing investment risk, providing a disciplined approach that helps investors stay focused on their long-term objectives.

Understanding your risk tolerance is essential in constructing a balanced portfolio. Everyone's comfort level with risk varies, influenced by age, financial goals, and personal circumstances. Risk assessment questionnaires serve as valuable tools in gauging your risk appetite. These questionnaires evaluate your reactions to market volatility, financial goals, and investment experience, offering insights into your risk profile. By matching your investment choices with your risk tolerance, you create a portfolio that aligns with both your financial objectives and emotional comfort. This harmony is crucial, as an investment strategy that complements your risk preference reduces anxiety and fosters confidence in your financial journey.

As life evolves, so too should your investment strategy. Periodic portfolio reviews and adjustments are vital to maintaining desired risk levels and ensuring your investments align with your changing goals. Life events, such as marriage, the birth of a child, or retirement, can significantly impact your risk tolerance. For example, as you approach retirement, you may wish to shift towards more conservative investments to preserve capital. Regularly revisiting your portfolio allows you to make informed adjustments, rebalancing your asset allocation to maintain the right mix of growth and security. This proactive strategy safeguards your investments and ensures your financial plan remains flexible and adaptable to life's changes.

A resilient investment strategy offers numerous benefits, particularly during economic uncertainty. Consider the case of a retiree who crafted a diversified portfolio with a balanced allocation of stocks, bonds, and alternative assets. During a market downturn, while some investors saw significant losses, this retiree's portfolio remained stable, thanks to the cushioning effect of diversification. The bonds provided steady income, while alternative investments offered growth opportunities, offsetting the volatility in the stock market. This example illustrates how a well-balanced portfolio can withstand economic shocks, providing peace of mind and financial security.

Reflection Exercise: Assessing and Adjusting Your Portfolio

Take a moment to reflect on the current state of your investment portfolio. Consider the following questions to evaluate its balance and resilience:

1. How diversified is your portfolio across different asset classes, such as stocks, bonds, and alternative investments?
2. Have you conducted a recent risk assessment to ensure your portfolio aligns with your current risk tolerance and financial goals?
3. Are there any life changes or upcoming milestones that may require adjustments to your investment strategy?

Regularly revisiting these questions will help you maintain a resilient portfolio, ensuring it remains aligned with your evolving financial landscape.

5.1 UNDERSTANDING AND MANAGING MARKET VOLATILITY

Market Volatility can be likened to the unpredictable waves of the ocean, sometimes calm and serene, other times turbulent and overwhelming. It refers to the fluctuations in market prices, which can significantly impact your investments and, by extension, your retirement plans. These price changes often stem from economic indicators, geopolitical events, or shifts in investor sentiment. When markets are volatile, the value of your investments can swing dramatically, affecting the overall worth of your retirement savings. This uncertainty can be unsettling, especially when retirement security is at stake. According to sources, volatility indexes, such as the VIX, provide a measure of market uncertainty, offering insights into investor expectations for future volatility.

Historically, we've witnessed periods of intense market volatility that have tested even the most seasoned investors. An example of how quickly market conditions can change is the 2008 financial crisis. During this time, asset prices plummeted, eroding the value of retirement portfolios and leaving many to reassess their economic strategies. Yet, these historical examples also offer lessons in resilience and recovery. Markets eventually rebounded, rewarding those who remained patient and committed to their long-term goals. Understanding these patterns allows you to approach market volatility with a sense of perspective, recognizing it as a natural element of investing rather than an insurmountable obstacle.

Managing your emotional response to volatility is crucial in making rational investment decisions. Investing psychology often uncovers emotional biases like fear and greed, which can impair judgment and lead to rash decisions. The instinct to sell and cut losses can be strong during a market downturn. However, this reaction often results in locking in losses rather than riding out the storm. To maintain composure, it's helpful to develop cognitive strategies that foster a calm and rational mindset. Practicing mindfulness, for example, can ground you in the present moment, helping to separate emotional reactions from logical decision-making. Additionally, reviewing your long-term goals can reinforce the importance of staying the course, even when market conditions are challenging.

When markets become unstable, there are specific actions you can take to protect your portfolio. Stop-loss orders, for instance, allow you to set predetermined prices at which your investments will be sold, limiting potential losses. Hedging techniques, such as options or futures, can also provide a buffer against market downturns by offsetting potential declines in asset values. Increasing your cash reserves is another prudent strategy, offering an economic cushion that can be used to seize opportunities or cover expenses without selling investments at a loss. These proactive measures can fortify your portfolio against volatility, preserving your financial security.

Consider the story of Ellen, a retiree who successfully navigated market volatility with a steady hand. Ellen's portfolio included a mix of equities and fixed-income securities, providing both growth potential and stability. During the market turbulence of 2008, she resisted the urge to sell her holdings, instead focusing on her long-term objectives. By maintaining her investment strategy and utilizing stop-loss orders to manage risk, Ellen emerged from the crisis with her wealth intact. Her experience highlights the importance of a disciplined approach, demonstrating how thoughtful planning and emotional resilience can weather volatile conditions.

Another example is Tomás, who learned to adapt his strategy in response to market changes. Initially, Tomás was overwhelmed by the rapid fluctuations in his portfolio's value. However, by working with a financial advisor, he developed a plan that incorporated hedging strategies and increased cash reserves. This approach gave Tomás the confidence to navigate volatility, enabling him to make informed decisions and maintain his financial stability. His journey underscores the value of professional guidance and strategic adjustments in managing market uncertainty.

5.2 THE ROLE OF BONDS AND BOND LADDERS IN RISK MANAGEMENT

In retirement planning, bonds play a pivotal role, offering a steady income stream while lowering your risk profile compared to stocks. Bonds are essentially loans you give to the government or corporations. In return, they promise to pay you interest over a set period. This interest, known as the bond yield, provides a predictable income source, making bonds an ideal choice for retirees seeking stability. Government bonds, often considered the safest, are backed by the full faith and credit of the issuing country, offering low-risk and modest returns. Municipal bonds, disseminated by state or local governments, can offer tax advantages, particularly if you reside in the issuing state. Corporate bonds, while riskier, typically offer higher yields, reflecting the greater risk of default compared to government-backed options. The interplay between bond yields and interest rates is crucial; as interest rates rise, bond prices tend to fall, impacting their market value but not their income potential if held to maturity.

Bond ladders present a strategic method for achieving income stability while mitigating interest rate risk. This approach involves purchasing bonds with staggered maturity dates, creating a ladder-like structure where bonds mature regularly. By doing so, you ensure a consistent flow of income as each bond matures, allowing you to reinvest the principal at current interest rates. This strategy reduces the risk of being locked into a single interest rate environment, providing flexibility and adaptability. In varying rate environments, bond ladders offer significant benefits. When rates rise, maturing bonds can be reinvested at higher yields, enhancing income. Conversely, in a declining rate environment, the ladder structure allows you to capture higher rates from previous investments while benefiting from capital gains on existing bonds. Real-life examples abound, with many retirees opting for bond ladders to secure a predictable income stream that aligns with their financial needs and market conditions.

Bonds also serve as a hedge against market volatility, preserving capital during stock market declines. A critical role in this protective function is the inverse association between bonds and interest rates. When stock markets falter, investors often flock to the safety of bonds, driving up their prices. This behavior can stabilize your portfolio's value, offsetting potential losses from equities. Including bonds in your investment mix thus enhances diversification, spreading risk across asset classes and reducing overall portfolio volatility. By balancing the growth potential of stocks with the stability of bonds, you build a resilient financial strategy that can withstand economic fluctuations.

When selecting bonds, it's important to consider the bond ratings and credit risks associated with each investment. Bond ratings, assigned by agencies like Moody's or Standard & Poor's, offer insights into the issuer's creditworthiness, guiding you in assessing the likelihood of default. Higher-rated bonds generally present lower risk but offer lower yields, while lower-rated, or "junk" bonds, provide higher returns at the expense of inflated risk.

Evaluating these ratings, alongside factors such as maturity date and coupon rate, helps you construct a bond ladder that aligns with your risk tolerance and income requirements. Tools for planning and maintaining bond ladders abound, ranging from online calculators to consultation with financial advisors, ensuring your ladder is optimally structured to meet your financial objectives.

In crafting a bond ladder, consider your investment horizon and income needs. Begin by determining the overall length of the ladder and the spacing between maturities, ensuring they align with your financial goals. Diversifying the types of bonds within the ladder, such as incorporating municipal, government, and corporate bonds, can further enhance stability and income potential. As bonds mature, reinvest the principal into new longer-term bonds, adapting to interest rate changes and adjusting the ladder as needed. This systematic approach provides predictable income and enhances your ability to navigate shifting economic landscapes. Integrating bonds and ladders into your retirement strategy will pave the way for financial security and peace of mind in your golden years.

5.3 INSURANCE STRATEGIES FOR RETIREMENT: BEYOND HEALTH COVERAGE

As you approach retirement, insurance becomes a vital tool in your financial safety net, extending its protective reach beyond traditional health coverage. One crucial aspect to consider is long-term care insurance. This type of insurance covers services that Medicare typically doesn't, such as assistance with daily living activities at home or in a nursing facility. By securing long-term care insurance, you can avoid depleting your savings on unexpected healthcare needs, preserving your assets for other retirement goals. It creates an extra layer of protection, safeguarding against significant claims that could otherwise jeopardize your financial stability. Both options play a critical role in fortifying your retirement plan against unforeseen expenses.

Insurance serves a strategic purpose in mitigating various financial risks. Annuities, for instance, can offer a stream of guaranteed income, acting as an economic anchor during retirement. This consistent income can alleviate the pressure on your other investments, allowing them to grow. At the same time, you enjoy a stable cash flow. Life insurance, too, holds strategic value for estate planning and wealth transfer. It ensures your loved ones receive monetary support, maintaining your legacy and fulfilling your intentions. Beyond protection, these insurance products can provide peace of mind, knowing that you've safeguarded against potential income disruptions and that your financial plan remains on course.

Selecting the right insurance policies requires careful evaluation. Begin by assessing the costs and benefits of each policy, ensuring they align with your financial needs and goals. It's essential to understand policy exclusions and limitations, as these can influence the extent of coverage. For example, some long-term care policies may not cover certain conditions or types of care, so clarity here is crucial. Seeking professional guidance and comparing various policies can aid in making informed decisions, ensuring you choose the coverage that best fits your circumstances. This process, though intricate, equips you with a tailored insurance plan that strengthens your retirement security.

Consider the story of Mary, a retiree who effectively leveraged insurance to bolster her financial security. Mary invested in long-term care insurance early, recognizing the potential impact of healthcare costs on her savings. When she later required in-home care, her policy covered a significant portion of the expenses, allowing her to maintain her lifestyle and preserve her assets. Another retiree, Jim, used an umbrella insurance policy to protect against a substantial liability claim. This foresight shielded his estate, ensuring his financial plans remained intact. When integrated thoughtfully into a retirement strategy, these examples illustrate how insurance can prevent financial ruin and enhance overall security.

In its many forms, insurance is more than a shield—it is a cornerstone of a well-rounded retirement plan. Understanding and utilizing the right products can mitigate risks and secure your financial future. As we've explored, insurance provides stability, offering solutions that protect against the uncertainties of life. Careful planning becomes an integral part of your strategy, supporting your goals and ensuring peace of mind. As we transition to the next chapter, we will explore how behavioral finance and emotional preparedness can further safeguard your retirement.

6

BEHAVIORAL FINANCE AND EMOTIONAL PREPAREDNESS

Envision walking into a lively marketplace filled with excitement. Every vendor is eager to catch your eye, boasting the best products at the best prices. This scene mirrors the investment world, where emotional biases often drive decisions, clouding judgment and leading to less-than-optimal financial outcomes. While capable of remarkable rationality, the human mind is susceptible to biases that skew our perceptions and influence our choices. Understanding these biases is crucial in retirement planning, where decisions made today have lasting implications for your future security.

6.1 OVERCOMING EMOTIONAL BIASES IN FINANCIAL DECISIONS

Among the most pervasive emotional biases is loss aversion, a reluctance to acknowledge and act on investments that are performing poorly. This bias stems from the discomfort associated with realizing losses, often leading investors to hold onto losing assets, hoping for a turnaround. This tendency can stall the reallocation of resources to more promising opportunities, ultimately impairing long-term returns. Overconfidence is another common bias, where individuals overestimate their financial acumen. This misplaced confidence can lead to risky investment decisions, as individuals believe they possess superior insight or information. The allure of outsmarting the market often backfires, resulting in losses that could have been avoided with a more measured approach.

Herd behavior, the inclination to follow the crowd in investment choices, further complicates decision-making. This bias is fueled by the fear of missing out or the assumption that the collective knows best. However, such behavior can lead to participation in speculative bubbles, where asset prices inflate beyond their intrinsic value, only to crash precipitously. The dot-com bubble of the late 1990s exemplifies this phenomenon, where irrational exuberance drove investors to pour money into technology stocks without due diligence. When the bubble burst, many faced substantial losses, underscoring the dangers of herd mentality in investment.

These biases can significantly impact retirement planning, leading to emotional decision-making and suboptimal financial outcomes. Emotional responses often override rational analysis, causing investors to sell in panic during market downturns or chase high returns without considering the associated risks. This bias-induced behavior can result in a misaligned portfolio, exposing individuals to unnecessary volatility or overly conservative positions that stifle growth. Recognizing these patterns is the first step in mitigating their effects and ensuring a more balanced approach to financial decision-making.

To counteract these biases, it is essential to cultivate mindfulness and self-awareness. Regularly engaging in mindfulness exercises can enhance your ability to identify and reflect on emotional triggers, allowing you to approach investment decisions objectively. Cognitive reframing, challenging and altering negative thought patterns, can also effectively combat bias-driven thoughts. For example, instead of focusing on the potential loss of selling a declining asset, reframe the decision as an opportunity to invest in a more promising avenue. By shifting your perspective, you can make decisions grounded in logic rather than emotion.

Case studies provide compelling evidence of individuals who have successfully managed their biases to improve financial outcomes. Consider the example of an investor who took proactive steps to recalibrate his strategy after experiencing significant losses due to overconfidence. By acknowledging his limitations, he sought the advice of a financial advisor and diversified his portfolio. This strategic adjustment minimized risk and enhanced returns, illustrating the power of informed decision-making. Another case highlights an investor who overcame herd behavior by conducting independent research and adhering to a disciplined investment plan. She maintained a stable portfolio that weathered market fluctuations by resisting the urge to follow market trends.

Reflection Exercise: Recognizing Your Biases

Take a moment to reflect on your investment decisions and identify any biases that may have influenced them. Consider the following questions:

1. Have you ever held onto a losing investment longer than advisable due to loss aversion?
2. Do you find yourself overconfident in your investment knowledge, leading to risky decisions?

3. Have you ever followed the crowd in investment choices, only to experience regret?

Reflecting on these questions can help you recognize patterns in your behavior and take steps to address them, paving the way for more rational and effective financial decision-making.

6.2 THE PSYCHOLOGY OF SPENDING: ALIGNING HABITS WITH GOALS

Consider a scenario where a stressful day at work leads to an impulsive shopping spree. The thrill of purchasing new items temporarily alleviates stress, but the reality of financial strain soon sets in. This cycle, often termed "retail therapy," underscores the emotional triggers that can drive spending behaviors, diverting resources from long-term goals. Stress isn't the only culprit; social influences also play a significant role. Keeping up with friends' spending habits or societal expectations can pressure individuals to spend beyond their means, compromising retirement savings. Recognizing these emotional and social triggers is the first step towards aligning spending habits with your retirement aspirations.

To create harmony between your spending and retirement goals, it's essential to cultivate mindful spending habits. Begin by establishing a budget that reflects not only your financial reality but also your values and aspirations. This involves differentiating between needs and wants, and prioritizing spending that supports your long-term objectives. Budgeting strategies like the 50/30/20 rule—allocating 50% of income to needs, 30% to wants, and 20% to savings—can provide a structured approach. By setting financial priorities aligned with what truly matters, you can make informed decisions that support both present enjoyment and future security.

Technology offers powerful tools to track and analyze your spending patterns. Finance apps, like Mint or YNAB (You Need A Budget), provide real-time insights into your expenditures, helping you identify areas where adjustments may be needed. These apps categorize spending, allowing you to see where your money goes each month and illustrate trends over time. They can also alert you to potential overspending, prompting timely interventions. Coupled with digital solutions, traditional methods like spending journals can enhance awareness. By recording each purchase and reflecting on the motivation behind it, you gain valuable insights into your habits, paving the way for meaningful change.

Consider the story of Alex, who transformed his financial outlook by realigning his spending with his retirement goals. Initially, Alex frequently indulged in impulse purchases, often justifying them as rewards for hard work. However, this behavior left him with little savings for his future. Recognizing the need for change, Alex began tracking his expenses using a finance app, which revealed the extent of his discretionary spending. Armed with this knowledge, he adopted a budget that prioritized savings, setting aside a fixed percentage of each paycheck for retirement. Over time, Alex saw a substantial increase in his savings, providing him peace of mind and a more straightforward path to financial security.

Another example is Maria, who successfully reduced her discretionary spending to bolster her retirement fund. Faced with a growing credit card balance, Maria decided to take control of her finances by implementing envelope budgeting—a cash-based system that limits spending to the cash you physically allocate for each category. This tangible method helped Maria curtail unnecessary expenses, redirecting funds toward her retirement savings. The discipline of physically managing her money changed her relationship with spending, transforming a source of stress into a tool for achieving financial independence. Maria's story illustrates the profound impact that mindful spending can have on retirement readiness, demonstrating that it's never too late to align habits with aspirations.

As you reflect on these examples, consider how you might apply similar approaches to your financial life. Identify emotional triggers that lead to unplanned spending and explore technology that can assist in creating a comprehensive view of your finances. By fostering awareness and discipline, you can transform your spending habits into a powerful ally as you journey toward a secure and fulfilling retirement.

6.3 PREPARING EMOTIONALLY FOR RETIREMENT: A BALANCED APPROACH

Retirement represents a significant life transition, often bringing the challenge of redefining one's identity. For many, work provides financial stability, a sense of purpose, and social interaction. With retirement, the roles that once defined you fade, leaving space that can sometimes feel daunting to fill. The sudden absence of daily responsibilities and the structure they provide can evoke feelings of loss. This identity shift is a natural part of the retirement process. Yet, it requires thoughtful navigation to ensure it becomes an opportunity for growth rather than a source of anxiety. While initially appealing, the increase in leisure time can lead to unease if not purposefully directed. It's essential to view this time as a canvas upon which to paint new experiences and pursuits, fostering a balanced and fulfilling lifestyle.

The emotional transition from a structured work life to the uncharted waters of retirement requires preparation and adaptation. It's beneficial to start exploring new hobbies and interests before retiring. This proactive approach helps ease the transition and provides continuity in daily life. Whether picking up photography, joining a local book club, or learning a new language, these activities can become pillars of your new routine. Building a robust support network is equally vital. Engaging with friends, family, or community groups can provide the social interaction that work once offered. Consider joining clubs based on your interests or volunteer organizations to connect with others who share similar passions. These networks not only enrich your life but also offer support and companionship, critical elements in navigating the emotional aspects of retirement.

Maintaining mental health during retirement is crucial for overall well-being and satisfaction. Keeping the mind active and engaged helps to ward off feelings of stagnation and boredom. Cognitive activities such as solving puzzles, reading, or taking online courses can help maintain mental sharpness. These activities stimulate the brain, fostering a sense of accomplishment and growth. Volunteer opportunities offer another avenue for maintaining mental and social engagement. Contributing your time and skills to causes you care about creates a sense of purpose and fulfillment. Volunteering benefits the community and enhances your well-being, providing a rewarding way to stay connected and active. It's about finding a balance that enriches your life and keeps your mind sharp.

Consider the story of David, a retiree who found joy and purpose after leaving his long-held career. Initially, David struggled with the loss of his professional identity, feeling adrift without the daily structure of work. However, he soon discovered a passion for woodworking, a hobby he had dabbled in during his youth. As he honed his skills, David began crafting furniture for friends and family, transforming his pastime into a fulfilling endeavor. This newfound focus not only occupied his hands but also reinvigorated his sense of self-worth and creativity. David's story is a testament to the power of embracing new interests and their positive impact on one's emotional well-being.

Another example is Helen, who found fulfillment in retirement by fostering a sense of community. After retiring from a demanding corporate job, Helen felt isolated and unsure of how to fill her days. She began to volunteer at a local animal shelter, where she found a profound sense of connection and purpose. Through her work, Helen forged new friendships with fellow volunteers and found immense joy in caring for the animals. This experience provided structure to her days and enriched her life with new relationships and a sense of belonging. Helen's journey highlights the importance of staying engaged and connected, illustrating how volunteering can transform retirement into a rewarding chapter of life.

6.4 BEHAVIORAL TRAPS: COMMON MISTAKES AND HOW TO AVOID THEM

In the complex landscape of retirement planning, behavioral traps often lurk just beneath the surface, waiting to derail even the most carefully crafted plans. One of the most common pitfalls is procrastination when updating financial plans. It's easy to postpone reviewing investments or recalibrating a budget, especially when life gets busy. However, neglecting these updates can lead to outdated strategies that no longer align with evolving goals or market conditions. Over time, this inaction can erode the value of savings, leaving you unprepared for the future. Another prevalent trap is panic selling during market downturns. When markets become volatile, the instinct to protect assets by selling them quickly can be overwhelming. Yet, such actions often lock in losses and forfeit potential recoveries, undermining long-term investment growth.

These behavioral missteps can have grave consequences for financial security. For instance, failing to review and adjust financial plans regularly can result in missed opportunities for growth and increased vulnerability to economic shifts. Without regular attention, a portfolio can drift from its intended allocation, exposing it to undue risk or stagnation. Panic selling, on the other hand, crystallizes losses and creates emotional distress. Watching hard-earned savings dwindle due to impulsive decisions can lead to regret and anxiety, further complicating financial recovery. The emotional toll of these mistakes often exacerbates their economic impact, perpetuating a cycle of reactive decision-making that harms long-term stability.

Establishing regular financial check-ins can be transformative to navigate these traps and maintain financial discipline. Schedule quarterly reviews of your investments and financial goals, treating them as fixed appointments in your calendar. This practice ensures you stay engaged with your monetary strategy, making timely adjustments as needed. Additionally, setting up automatic investments and savings can help mitigate the effects of procrastination. By automating contributions to retirement accounts or investment portfolios, you remove the burden of manual decision-making and foster consistent growth. Automated systems work silently in the background, leveraging the power of compounding to build wealth over time without requiring constant oversight.

Consider the transformative journey of Emma, who overcame the challenges of procrastination with deliberate action. Initially overwhelmed by the complexities of financial planning, Emma found herself repeatedly postponing critical updates. Realizing the need for change, she committed to quarterly financial reviews, setting aside dedicated time to evaluate her portfolio and align it with her evolving goals. This proactive approach empowered Emma to seize new investment opportunities and adjust her strategy in response to market changes, ultimately enhancing her financial security. Her story underscores the importance of regular engagement with one's economic plans, demonstrating how consistent attention can mitigate the risks of procrastination.

Another illustrative example is Jack, who learned the perils of panic selling firsthand. During a period of market turbulence, Jack hastily sold a significant portion of his investments, fearing further losses. However, as the market rebounded, he was left with diminished holdings and missed gains. Jack adopted a disciplined approach to avoid repeating this mistake, setting predefined criteria for investment choices based on market conditions rather than emotions. This strategy allowed him to confidently navigate future downturns, preserving his assets and fostering resilience. Jack's experience highlights the critical role of strategic planning in overcoming behavioral traps, emphasizing the value of structure and foresight.

By understanding and addressing these behavioral traps, you can protect your economic future and ensure your retirement plans remain on track. In the next chapter, we will explore the role of real-life applications and case studies in retirement planning, exploring how lessons from others' experiences can inform and refine your own strategies.

7

REAL-LIFE APPLICATIONS AND CASE STUDIES

Imagine retirement planning as a complex puzzle, each piece representing a crucial decision that shapes your financial future. The stories of those who have navigated this intricate process offer invaluable insights and inspiration. In this chapter, we explore the journeys of individuals who have strategically aligned their retirement plans with their life goals, balancing traditional and modern investment methods to achieve financial security. These narratives illuminate the path to successful retirement and provide practical lessons that you can apply to your planning.

7.1 LEARNING FROM SUCCESS: CASE STUDIES OF STRATEGIC RETIREMENT PLANNING

Consider the story of Marco and Lisa, who exemplify the art of balancing traditional and modern investment strategies. In their early 40s, Marco and Lisa realized that relying solely on conventional retirement accounts might not suffice to secure their desired future. They began by maximizing contributions to their

401(k)s and Roth IRAs, ensuring a solid foundation. However, they also recognized the potential of modern financial tools like Bitcoin. By allocating a small percentage of their portfolio to this digital asset, they diversified their investments, mitigating risk while enhancing growth potential. This strategic blend of old and new allowed them to capitalize on the strengths of each approach, resulting in a robust retirement plan that aligned with their long-term goals.

Another inspiring example is Sarah, an entrepreneur who seamlessly integrated her business proceeds into her retirement strategy. Sarah's journey began with the realization that her business success could be a powerful catalyst for her financial future. Rather than drawing a substantial salary, she reinvested profits into the business while also channeling funds into a SEP IRA, taking advantage of its generous contribution limits. This decision secured her business's growth and fortified her retirement savings. As her business flourished, Sarah diversified her investments further, incorporating real estate and annuities to ensure a stable income stream in retirement. Her ability to see the interconnectedness of her business and retirement plans enabled her to build a comprehensive strategy catering to present and future needs.

Key strategies underpinning these success stories revolve around diversification and foresight. Diversified portfolios like Marco's and Lisa's reduce risk by spreading investments across various asset classes. This approach reduces exposure to market volatility and enhances growth potential. As demonstrated by Sarah's proactive approach, early planning and consistent contributions play a crucial role. By starting early and maintaining a disciplined savings regimen, she maximized the benefits of compound interest, creating a substantial nest egg over time.

Common traits among successful planners include discipline and adaptability. Whether sticking to a budget or adjusting investment strategies in response to market changes, these individuals steadfastly commit to their goals. They remain open to new ideas and technologies, embracing opportunities that align with their values and objectives. This flexibility allows them to navigate financial landscapes confidently, knowing they can adapt to life's inevitable twists and turns.

The actionable takeaways from these stories are explicit. Aligning investments with life goals is paramount. By identifying your core values, you can make better decisions that align with your future goals. Continuous education and financial literacy are equally vital. Staying informed about financial trends and tools empowers you to make strategic choices, enhancing your ability to achieve a secure and fulfilling retirement.

Reflection Exercise: Crafting Your Personal Retirement Strategy

Take a moment to reflect on your own financial journey. Consider the following questions to help shape your retirement strategy.

1. How can you balance traditional retirement tools with modern investment opportunities?
2. What role do your current and future income sources play in your retirement plan?
3. How can continuous learning enhance your financial decision-making processes?

Reflecting on these questions can guide you in creating a personalized strategy that aligns with your aspirations, ensuring a secure and rewarding retirement.

7.2 AVOIDING PITFALLS: LESSONS FROM FINANCIAL MISSTEPS

Retirement planning has potential pitfalls that can undermine even the most carefully crafted plans. Consider the case of Janet, a retiree who found herself in a precarious situation due to an oversight in healthcare planning. Like many, Janet underestimated her future medical expenses, assuming that Medicare would cover most costs. However, as unexpected health issues arose, she faced mounting out-of-pocket expenses that quickly depleted her savings. This financial strain threatened her retirement security and caused significant emotional stress, overshadowing her golden years with worry and uncertainty. Janet's experience underscores the critical importance of planning for healthcare needs. This lesson resonates with many retirees who face similar challenges.

In another scenario, we meet Tom, an investor who took excessive risks during market highs. Fueled by optimism and the allure of quick gains, Tom heavily invested in a single, volatile stock. Initially, his portfolio flourished, and his confidence soared. However, when the market corrected, the stock plummeted, eroding a significant portion of his retirement savings. This impacted his financial security and led to considerable stress and regret over his decisions. Tom's story highlights the dangers of overreliance on high-risk investments and the need for diversification to safeguard against market volatility.

Examining these missteps reveals common warning signs and pitfalls that can derail retirement plans. Overreliance on a single income source, whether a specific investment or Social Security, can leave individuals vulnerable to financial instability. Additionally, failing to adjust spending in response to market changes can exacerbate financial woes. When income diminishes, or expenses rise unexpectedly, maintaining the same level of spending can quickly lead to depleted savings. Recognizing these red flags early and taking proactive steps to address them is crucial in maintaining long-term financial security.

To mitigate these risks, consider implementing strategies that fortify your retirement plan against unforeseen challenges. Regular financial reviews and assessments can help identify vulnerabilities and ensure your strategy aligns with your current circumstances and goals. You can make informed decisions about adjusting asset allocations or exploring new investment opportunities by periodically evaluating your portfolio. This proactive approach helps maintain balance and enhances your ability to adapt to changing market conditions.

Building a robust emergency fund is another vital step in safeguarding your financial future. This fund serves as a financial cushion, providing the resources needed to cover unexpected expenses without tapping into your retirement savings. Aim to save enough to cover three to six months' living expenses, offering peace of mind and financial stability during unforeseen events. An emergency fund allows you to weather short-term financial storms, preserving your long-term savings for their intended purpose.

The stories of Janet and Tom serve as poignant reminders of the complexities and challenges in retirement planning. By learning from these experiences, you can take actionable steps to avoid similar pitfalls and enhance your financial security. Whether it's accounting for healthcare costs, diversifying your investments, or establishing an emergency fund, these strategies empower you to navigate the uncertainties of retirement with confidence and resilience. As you reflect on these lessons, consider how they might inform and strengthen your retirement strategy, guiding you toward a more secure and fulfilling future.

7.3 THE POWER OF PERSONALIZATION: TAILORING STRATEGIES TO INDIVIDUAL NEEDS

In the realm of retirement planning, personalization is a powerful tool that can transform a generic financial strategy into one that aligns with your unique circumstances. Tailoring your retirement plan involves more than choosing investments; it requires a profound understanding of your personal goals, risk tolerance, and values. By adapting asset allocation to your comfort with risk, you create a portfolio that seeks growth and allows you to sleep soundly at night. This customization ensures that your investments reflect your financial aspirations and emotional resilience to market fluctuations. Incorporating personal values into your financial decisions adds another layer of meaning and purpose. Whether it's prioritizing sustainability through environmentally conscious investments or supporting companies that align with your ethical beliefs, aligning your investments with your values can lead to greater satisfaction and fulfillment. This approach transforms retirement planning from a mere financial exercise into a reflection of who you are and what matters most to you.

Real-world examples illuminate the transformative potential of personalized retirement strategies. Consider Emily, a single parent who prioritized education savings for her children while planning for her retirement. Emily understood that her children's future was a top priority, so she tailored her investment strategy to balance growth and safety. She allocated funds to a 529 plan, ensuring her children could access education without compromising her financial security. This thoughtful approach allowed Emily to fulfill her dual responsibilities, demonstrating how aligning investments with personal values can lead to a successful and satisfying retirement plan. Then there's George, a retiree who focused on charitable giving as an integral part of his legacy. George had always been passionate about supporting local charities and wanted this passion to continue into his retirement. He could contribute to his favorite causes by setting up a donor-advised fund while enjoying tax benefits. This strategy fulfilled his philanthropic goals and provided a sense of purpose and connection to his community. George's experience illustrates how incorporating personal values into retirement planning can create a fulfilling and impactful legacy.

The benefits of flexibility and adaptability in retirement planning cannot be overstated. Life is unpredictable, and your retirement plan should be able to evolve in response to changes in your health, family, or financial situation. This adaptability ensures that your plan remains relevant and effective, regardless of what life throws your way. Leveraging technology can facilitate real-time financial adjustments, allowing you to make informed decisions quickly and efficiently. Financial planning software and apps will enable you to monitor your investments, track your spending, and adjust your strategy. This technological edge empowers you to adapt to changing circumstances, ensuring your retirement plan remains aligned with your goals.

To create a personalized retirement plan, start by conducting a personal financial audit. This involves assessing your current financial situation, identifying your priorities, and understanding your goals. Consider your income sources, expenses, debts, and assets to view your financial landscape comprehensively. Once you have a clear picture, set specific, measurable goals aligning with your priorities. Whether achieving financial independence, traveling the world, or leaving a legacy for your loved ones, having clear goals will guide your investment decisions and keep you focused on what truly matters. As you tailor your retirement plan, remember that personalization is ongoing. Regularly revisit your goals and adjust your strategy as your circumstances change. By embracing personalization, you can create a retirement plan that secures your financial future and enriches your life with purpose and fulfillment.

7.4 DIVERSE PATHS TO RETIREMENT SUCCESS: STORIES ACROSS DEMOGRAPHICS

In the diverse tapestry of retirement planning, individual experiences weave a rich narrative. Consider a young professional named Alex, who ventured into the tech world with a keen eye on financial growth. Working in a sector that thrives on innovation, Alex leveraged technology not just in his career but also in his investment strategy. By automating his savings and employing robo-advisors, he efficiently managed his portfolio. This approach saved him time and allowed him to capitalize on market opportunities with agility. His tech-savvy background enabled him to explore cryptocurrencies, adding a modern twist to his traditional investments. Through this blend of cutting-edge tools and strategic foresight, Alex exemplifies how the digital age offers unique avenues for building wealth, especially for those willing to embrace new technologies.

In stark contrast, we meet Eleanor, a retiree whose journey took a different turn. After decades in education, Eleanor found herself yearning for more than leisure. She reignited her passion for art, transforming it into a second career. Setting up a small studio, she began teaching art classes and selling her work online.

This venture supplemented her retirement income and infused her life with renewed purpose and connection to her community. Eleanor's story highlights the power of aligning one's passions with financial goals, showcasing that retirement can be a time of reinvention and creativity. Her saga emphasizes the significance of flexibility and the willingness to pursue new paths, regardless of age.

As we look closer, it becomes apparent that diverse backgrounds bring unique challenges and opportunities to retirement planning. Many older adults face the difficult challenge of planning for their later years, where time constraints necessitate more aggressive saving and investment strategies. This demographic may grapple with healthcare costs, a significant concern that requires meticulous planning and foresight. Socioeconomic status further influences retirement strategies, with dual-income households enjoying more significant potential for wealth accumulation. In these scenarios, effective communication and joint financial planning are vital in maximizing resources and achieving shared goals.

The creativity and resilience of diverse planners shine through in various adaptations and solutions. Community based support systems have emerged as vital resources for retirees, offering a shared knowledge and assistance network. These systems foster collaboration and provide a safety net, particularly for those without traditional family structures. Additionally, the gig economy has opened new income streams for many, allowing retirees to engage in flexible work that aligns with their skills and interests. Whether driving for a rideshare company or freelancing in a specialized field, these opportunities enable individuals to stay active and financially engaged without the constraints of a full-time job.

Despite the varied paths and experiences, universal principles underpin successful retirement planning across all demographics. Planning for long-term healthcare needs is paramount, as it safeguards against unforeseen medical expenses that can erode savings. Balancing risk and security in investments remains a cornerstone of financial stability, ensuring that portfolios are robust enough to weather market fluctuations while still generating growth. These themes transcend individual circumstances, emphasizing the importance of a holistic financial planning approach that considers immediate needs and future aspirations.

As we reflect on these various narratives, it is evident that retirement planning must be tailored to individual circumstances. Each individual's path is shaped by many factors, from personal passions to economic realities. By embracing the unique elements that define our lives, we can craft retirement strategies that secure our financial future and enrich our lives with purpose and fulfillment. The following chapter will delve into healthcare planning and insurance options, further equipping you with the tools to navigate the complexities of retirement with confidence.

8

HEALTHCARE PLANNING AND INSURANCE OPTIONS

In retirement planning, healthcare is a critical pillar, often surpassed by the more immediate concerns of financial savings and investment strategies. Yet, as we age, the intricacies of healthcare become ever more relevant, demanding our attention and understanding. Imagine healthcare planning as a safety net, intricately woven with threads of foresight and caution, ready to catch you should unexpected medical needs arise. Navigating healthcare in retirement requires not just awareness of costs but insight into the systems that support your well-being. With its multifaceted offerings, Medicare forms the backbone of this safety net, and understanding its components is crucial for maximizing your benefits.

Medicare is divided into four primary components, each serving a distinct role in healthcare coverage. Part A, known as hospital insurance, covers inpatient hospital stays, skilled nursing facilities care, hospice services, and home health care. Most people don't pay a premium for Part A because they've already contributed to Medicare taxes during their working years. Part B, known as medical insurance, covers doctor visits, outpatient care, medical equipment, and preventive services. Unlike Part A, Part B requires a monthly premium adjusted based on income. Part C, known as Medicare Advantage, offers an alternative way to receive your Medicare benefits. Medicare-approved private companies often provide extra benefits like vision, hearing, and dental coverage. However, they typically require you to use a network of doctors and hospitals. Part D provides prescription drug coverage, helping lower the cost of needed medications. It's important to note that Part D requires a separate premium and can be added to Original Medicare or some Medicare Advantage Plans. Understanding these components allows you to tailor your coverage to your specific health needs and financial situation.

Enrollment in Medicare is a critical step that requires careful timing to avoid unnecessary penalties. Missing this window can result in penalties that increase your premiums for Part B and Part D. Special Enrollment Periods (SEPs) may apply if you or your spouse are still working and covered by a group health plan, allowing you to delay enrollment without a penalty. However, you could face a late enrollment penalty if you delay enrolling in Part B or Part D without creditable coverage. This penalty is a permanent increase in your premium, calculated based on the length of time you were eligible but not enrolled. Therefore, understanding these enrollment periods and planning ahead can save you significant costs over time.

Choosing the right Medicare plan involves evaluating your health needs and financial circumstances. Cost, coverage, and provider networks should be carefully considered. Original Medicare allows flexibility in choosing healthcare providers that accept Medicare. In contrast, Medicare Advantage Plans may restrict you to their network. The Medicare Plan Finder tool is valuable for comparing plans, helping you understand the differences in coverage and out-of-pocket costs. Additionally, reviewing the plan's formulary (the list of covered drugs) and ensuring your preferred doctors are in-network can prevent unexpected expenses. Personalized assistance is also available through Medicare's helpline, which provides guidance for making informed decisions.

To complement Medicare, supplemental insurance options like Medigap can provide additional security by filling the gaps in coverage. Private companies deliver Medigap policies and assist in covering some healthcare costs that Original Medicare does not include, such as co-payments, coinsurance, and deductibles. There are assorted Medigap plans, each providing varying levels of coverage. Some plans, such as Plan F and Plan G, provide comprehensive benefits. However, Plan F is only available to those who qualified for Medicare before January 1, 2020. Cost considerations vary by plan type and state, as Medigap policies are standardized differently across states. When evaluating Medigap options, consider your health needs, budget, and the level of coverage you desire. Medigap can provide peace of mind by reducing out-of-pocket expenses and ensuring you have access to the care you need.

8.1 LONG-TERM CARE INSURANCE: A CRITICAL COMPONENT OF PLANNING

As we contemplate the future, the prospect of needing extended care becomes more likely. Long-term care insurance (LTCI) protects against the substantial costs associated with services that Medicare does not cover. These services may include help with everyday activities, such as bathing and dressing, as well as more comprehensive care in nursing homes or assisted living facilities. Long-term care planning is about more than just anticipating the possibility of needing such assistance; it is about ensuring that these expenses do not deplete your financial resources. By having an LTCI policy, you gain a measure of economic security, knowing you have a plan to manage the high costs of extended care. This foresight can relieve the burden on family members, allowing you to maintain your independence and dignity even as your care needs evolve.

When considering long-term care insurance, several factors influence the cost and coverage of a policy. Age and health status at the time of purchase are significant determinants. Typically, younger and healthier people receive the lowest premiums. Insurers assess your health through underwriting, which may include a review of your medical history and possibly a health exam. Another critical aspect to consider is the policy's benefit period, which defines the length of time benefits will be paid. Policies may offer benefit periods ranging from two years to lifetime coverage. Additionally, the daily benefit amount, or the maximum dollar amount the policy will pay daily, must align with the prevailing care costs in your area. Balancing these features with your budget is essential, ensuring the policy provides adequate coverage without becoming financially burdensome.

Finding the ideal long-term care policy requires a methodical approach. Start by comparing insurers, as policies and pricing can vary significantly between companies. Reputation and financial stability are important; you want an insurer that can pay claims well into the future. Examine policy terms closely, paying attention to what is covered and any exclusions. Understanding the triggers for benefit eligibility is paramount. Most policies require a physician's certification that you are unable to perform a specified amount of basic self-care tasks such as getting dressed or eating meals, often referred to as daily living activities (ADLs), or that you require supervision due to cognitive impairment. These triggers determine when you can begin receiving benefits, so ensure they are clearly defined and meet your expectations. Consulting a financial advisor or insurance specialist can provide valuable insights as you navigate these choices, helping you customize a policy that meets your needs and goals.

Consider the story of Roland and Katica, a couple who wisely invested in long-term care insurance in their early 60s. They recognized that, statistically, they would likely need some form of long-term care and wanted to preserve their retirement savings for their intended purposes. When Katica was diagnosed with a chronic illness in her 70s, their insurance policy covered the cost of in-home care, allowing her to remain in familiar surroundings with the support she needed. This coverage alleviated the financial strain on their savings, and they were able to continue enjoying their retirement without the stress of mounting care costs. Their experience underscores the importance of planning ahead and the peace of mind that a well-chosen policy can provide.

In another instance, consider Leo, who faced significant expenses when his father required nursing home care. Having witnessed the financial impact firsthand, Leo decided to secure long-term care insurance for himself and his wife, despite their current good health. This proactive step ensured they would have the resources to cover potential future care needs without compromising their financial security. Leo's decision highlights the value of learning from experience and the foresight required to protect oneself against unforeseen challenges.

8.2 MANAGING HEALTHCARE COSTS: STRATEGIES FOR FINANCIAL PROTECTION

Healthcare costs become a significant concern as you approach retirement, often representing a substantial portion of your budget. It's crucial to understand the typical expenses you may face. Premiums for health insurance can be a consistent outlay, while deductibles must be met before your insurance kicks in fully. Out-of-pocket expenses can add up quickly, including co-payments for doctor visits and prescription drugs. For those requiring ongoing medication, even with prescription drug plans, the co-payments can strain finances. An additional burden comes from the costs associated with long-term care facilities, which can be exorbitantly high. These facilities provide necessary services for those who need assistance with daily activities. However, the costs can deplete savings if not planned adequately. Understanding these potential expenses is the first step in crafting a financial strategy that protects your resources.

To manage these healthcare costs effectively, several strategies should be considered. One approach is setting aside funds in a Health Savings Account (HSA), which offers tax advantages that can significantly offset medical expenses. HSAs allow you to save money and make withdrawals for qualified medical expenses tax-free. This makes them a powerful tool for managing healthcare costs in retirement. Another strategy is to be mindful of the healthcare providers you choose. Costs can vary greatly between in-network and out-of-network providers. By ensuring your care is within your insurance network, you can avoid unnecessary expenses and make the most of your coverage. Creating a detailed budget that anticipates these costs will help you manage and allocate your resources effectively, ensuring that healthcare expenses do not derail your financial stability.

There are various tools and resources available to help reduce healthcare expenses. Patient assistance programs presented by pharmaceutical companies can lower the cost of prescription medications, sometimes significantly. These programs are often income-based but can provide crucial support for those who qualify. Negotiating medical bills is another avenue to explore. Healthcare providers are often open to negotiating payment plans or reducing costs if you cannot pay the total amount upfront. Communicating with providers about your financial situation and exploring all available options is important. These strategies can alleviate the burden of healthcare costs, enabling you to allocate your savings where they are most needed.

Consider the story of a retiree named Helena, who effectively managed her healthcare costs through strategic planning. Helena contributed to her HSA throughout her working years, allowing her to accumulate a substantial fund by retirement. This financial cushion enabled her to cover significant out-of-pocket medical expenses without dipping into her retirement savings. She also diligently ensured that all her medical care was provided within her insurance network, minimizing unexpected costs. Helena's prudent planning provided her with peace of mind and financial security, allowing her to focus on enjoying her retirement without the stress of looming medical bills. Her experience underscores the importance of proactive healthcare cost management.

Another example is Robert, who made the most of his Medicare benefits to control healthcare costs. Robert took the time to carefully evaluate his Medicare options, selecting a plan that provided comprehensive coverage for his specific health needs. By optimizing his Medicare plan, he reduced his out-of-pocket expenses significantly. Additionally, Robert utilized patient assistance programs to lower his prescription drug costs, further easing his financial burden. His strategic approach to healthcare planning allowed him to maintain financial stability while ensuring access to the necessary medical care. Robert's story highlights the value of informed decision-making and its impact on managing healthcare expenses in retirement.

8.3 INTEGRATING HEALTH AND WEALTH: A COMPREHENSIVE VIEW

Health and financial security are two sides of the same coin, particularly as you approach retirement. Proactive health planning is not just about medical check-ups; it's about laying a foundation for overall retirement security. Preventive care and healthy lifestyle choices can greatly decrease healthcare expenses and enhance quality of life. Consistent exercise, regular health screenings, and a nutritious diet are essential for your future well-being. These actions can prevent chronic conditions from developing or worsening, reducing the financial burden of managing such situations. Chronic health issues often require long-term treatment and medication, adding to your expenses and potentially depleting your retirement savings prematurely. Hence, integrating health-conscious decisions into your lifestyle is as crucial as any financial strategy.

Aligning healthcare decisions with your financial goals is a strategic move. Creating a health-focused retirement budget allows you to anticipate and allocate funds for potential medical expenses. This involves estimating future healthcare costs based on your current health status and potential changes as you age. Consider what percentage of your retirement income will be dedicated to healthcare, and adjust other expenses accordingly. Balancing healthcare costs with other financial priorities ensures that your savings support both your health needs and lifestyle desires. For instance, if you foresee higher healthcare costs, you might decide to downsize your living arrangements to free up funds. This balance is pivotal to maintaining monetary stability without sacrificing well-being.

Holistic planning approaches offer distinct advantages by integrating health and wealth strategies into a unified plan. Coordinating health insurance with investment strategies can maximize the efficiency of your savings. For example, choosing a high-deductible health plan paired with a Health Savings Account (HSA) allows for tax-free contributions that grow over time, providing a dedicated fund for healthcare expenses. Utilizing financial advisors who understand the nuances of health-related planning can also enhance your strategy. These professionals can help you make informed decisions that align with your health necessities and financial aspirations, ensuring a comprehensive approach to retirement planning.

Consider the story of Anna, who took a holistic approach to her retirement planning. Anna worked with her financial advisor to integrate her health and financial goals, ensuring they complemented each other. She opted for a high-deductible health plan and maximized her HSA contributions, allowing her savings to grow tax free. Anna also prioritized preventive care and healthy living, reducing her risk of chronic conditions and associated costs. This proactive approach enabled her to maintain her health and financial security, illustrating the power of a well-coordinated plan. Anna's experience highlights the importance of viewing health and wealth as interconnected components of a successful retirement strategy.

In another example, consider James, who balanced his healthcare needs with financial aspirations by leveraging technology and professional advice. James used health-tracking apps to monitor his well-being and adjusted his lifestyle based on the insights they provided. Additionally, he worked closely with his financial advisor to align his investment strategy with his health goals. By doing so, James ensured that his financial resources were structured to support his long-term health, allowing him to pursue his passions without financial constraints. His story demonstrates that integrating health and wealth planning can enhance economic security and quality of life in retirement.

In conclusion, integrating health and wealth planning is not just about managing expenses; it's about guaranteeing that your golden years are as fulfilling and worry-free as possible. By aligning these two critical aspects of life, you complete a robust framework supporting your financial and personal well-being. As we move forward, we will explore how these principles can be applied to risk management and financial security, helping your retirement plan remain strong amidst life's uncertainties.

9

BUDGETING, EXPENSE MANAGEMENT, AND LIFESTYLE

Imagine embarking on retirement not as a retreat from life's demands but as a new chapter filled with possibilities. The cornerstone of a fulfilling retirement is a sustainable budget that manages both your needs and desires. This financial roadmap requires thoughtful consideration and balance, ensuring long-term security without forgoing life's pleasures. A well-structured budget supports your financial stability, enabling you to enjoy the retirement you envision. You can prioritize what truly matters by distinguishing between essential and discretionary spending.

The process begins with identifying and categorizing your expenses. Fixed expenses like housing, healthcare, and utilities are non-negotiable necessities. These are the pillars of your financial foundation, supporting your daily life. Variable expenses, such as groceries and transportation, require careful monitoring to remain within your planned limits. Discretionary expenses, including travel, hobbies, and dining out, are where your personal enjoyment comes into play. These are flexible and can be revised based on your financial situation. Differentiating between these categories helps you allocate your resources effectively, balancing your budget to meet obligations and aspirations.

One effective budgeting technique, previously mentioned in Chapter 6, is the 50/30/20 rule, popularized by Senator Elizabeth Warren. This method divides your income into 50% for needs, 30% for wants, and 20% for savings. Needs encompass essentials like housing and healthcare, ensuring your basic requirements are met. Wants include non-essential but enriching expenses, allowing room for leisure and enjoyment. Savings focus on future security, building a cushion for unexpected events, and retirement goals. This straightforward framework offers a balanced approach, though it can be adjusted to conform to your circumstances. For instance, if you have a higher income, you may decide to allocate more towards savings, enhancing your financial resilience.

Another approach is zero-based budgeting, which maximizes resource allocation by assigning every dollar a purpose. This method requires you to account for all income, ensuring each expense is justified and aligned with your goals. While this approach demands diligence, it can lead to greater financial clarity and control. By evaluating your expenses regularly, you ensure your spending aligns with your priorities, allowing for adjustments as needs change. Both techniques emphasize intentional spending, encouraging you to make informed decisions that reflect your values and aspirations.

Flexibility is crucial in a successful budget, allowing you to adapt to life's uncertainties. Economic changes, such as inflation or rising healthcare costs, may necessitate adjustments in your spending plan. By incorporating unexpected expenses into your financial strategy, you can mitigate their impact without derailing your long-term goals. Periodic budget reviews help you stay on track, providing opportunities to reassess your priorities and make necessary changes. This adaptability ensures your budget remains a reliable guide, supporting your lifestyle while safeguarding your future.

Visual Element: Budgeting Checklist

A helpful tool for maintaining a sustainable budget is a budgeting checklist. Use the following guide to ensure all aspects of your financial plan are accounted for:

- **Essential Expenses:** Confirm all fixed expenses are covered, including housing, utilities, and healthcare.
- **Variable Expenses:** Monitor groceries, transportation, and other variable costs, adjusting as needed.
- **Discretionary Expenses:** Review leisure spending, ensuring it aligns with your financial goals.
- **Savings:** Verify savings contributions meet your retirement and emergency fund targets.
- **Regular Reviews:** Schedule periodic budget assessments to adjust for changes in income or expenses.
- **Emergency Fund:** Maintain a sufficient reserve for unexpected costs, reinforcing your financial security.

By following this checklist, you can maintain a balanced and flexible budget, supporting both immediate needs and future aspirations.

9.1 EXPENSE MANAGEMENT: TOOLS AND TECHNIQUES FOR FINANCIAL CLARITY

Technology has transformed how we keep tabs on our finances when managing expenses. Digital tools like personal finance apps provide real-time spending tracking, offering instant insights into where your money goes. Apps like Mint or Simplifi by Quicken categorize your expenses, alerting you to overspending in specific areas. These apps offer the convenience of monitoring your finances from your smartphone, ensuring you always remain aware of your financial health. They automatically update your spending, saving precious time and effort by linking to your bank accounts and credit cards. Budgeting software offers a more detailed analysis, enabling you to dive deeper into your financial habits. Programs like YNAB (You Need a Budget) allow you to plan every dollar, aligning your spending with your financial goals. These tools help you create a structured financial plan, providing clarity and direction in managing your expenses.

To effectively manage and reduce expenses without sacrificing your quality of life, consider strategies that focus on negotiating and cutting unnecessary costs. Start by scrutinizing recurring bills. Many services, such as cable or internet providers, are open to negotiation. Simply calling and asking for a better rate can lead to significant savings. Evaluate your subscriptions and memberships, canceling those you no longer use or need. For discretionary spending, practice mindfulness in your purchases. Before purchasing something, ask yourself if it matches your financial priorities or fulfills a want rather than a need. Small changes, like dining out less often or making homemade coffee, can add up over time. Embrace the idea of finding joy in experiences that don't require spending, such as enjoying nature or spending time with loved ones.

Creating a robust expense management plan involves setting clear spending limits and diligently monitoring adherence. Begin by determining realistic spending caps for various categories, ensuring they align with your overall financial strategy. Regularly review your expenditure to ensure compliance with these limits. Conducting periodic expense audits can reveal areas where adjustments are needed. During an audit, analyze your spending patterns, identifying potential savings without compromising your lifestyle. This exercise helps to keep you on track and adaptable, allowing you to refine your plan as needed. Maintaining a disciplined approach to managing outflows ensures that your financial resources are allocated efficiently.

Consider the story of Margaret, a retiree who successfully optimized her expense management through disciplined tracking. By using a finance app, she gained visibility into her spending habits. Margaret discovered she was spending more on dining out than anticipated, prompting her to set a weekly limit. She found satisfaction in cooking meals at home, enjoying the process and the savings. Another example is Jack, who used budgeting software to streamline his finances. He conducted regular expense audits, uncovering unnecessary expenses like unused subscriptions. By eliminating these costs, Jack could allocate more funds towards his travel goals, enhancing his retirement experience. These stories exemplify how effective expense management can bring financial clarity and fulfillment.

In the pursuit of financial clarity, these tools and techniques offer a pathway to understanding and controlling your financial landscape. They empower you to make informed decisions, aligning your spending with your values and goals. By embracing technology and adopting disciplined strategies, you can achieve a balanced financial life, ensuring your resources are directed toward what truly matters. Whether it's through negotiating costs, setting spending limits, or conducting audits, the key lies in maintaining a proactive approach to managing your expenses.

9.2 LIFESTYLE ADJUSTMENTS: FINANCIAL PLANNING FOR LIFE CHANGES

Transitioning from working life to retirement is more than just an escape from the 9-to-5 grind; it requires a significant shift in how you approach your finances. The certainty of a regular paycheck gives way to a fixed income, often requiring a reevaluation of spending patterns. This shift necessitates a strategic approach to financial planning, ensuring that your resources align with your new reality. As you enter this phase, your spending may lean more toward leisure and travel activities, which you might have postponed during your working years. Whether exploring new destinations or indulging in hobbies, these pursuits demand thoughtful budgeting to avoid straining your financial resources. Understanding these new spending patterns is crucial because they can influence how you allocate your retirement income, ensuring you enjoy your newfound freedom without financial stress.

Everyday life changes during retirement often necessitate financial adaptation. Relocation or downsizing, for instance, can offer cost efficiencies, freeing up funds for other priorities. Downsizing to a smaller home or relocating to a lower-cost community can significantly lower expenses, allowing you to redirect savings toward travel or personal interests. On the other hand, changes in family dynamics, such as becoming a caregiver, can profoundly impact your financial planning. This shift might require you to adjust your priorities and allocate resources differently, ensuring you meet personal and family obligations. Recognizing these potential changes early can help you prepare financially and maintain stability even as your circumstances evolve.

Planning for these lifestyle adjustments involves proactive strategies to manage the financial impacts of life transitions. One practical approach is creating contingency plans for unexpected events. By setting aside funds specifically for unforeseen circumstances, you can guarantee that your financial plan remains intact despite surprises. This reserve acts as a buffer, providing peace of mind and preventing you from having to dip into your primary savings. Additionally, incorporating lifestyle goals into your long-term financial plans allows you to align your spending with your aspirations. Whether planning for annual vacations or setting aside funds for new experiences, these goals should be woven into your financial strategy, providing direction and purpose to your retirement.

Real-life examples of successful lifestyle adjustments offer valuable insights into how retirees have managed financial planning amidst significant life changes. Consider the story of Lucas and Nad'a, who relocated to a coastal town known for its affordability and vibrant community life. They significantly reduced their living costs by downsizing from their suburban home to a smaller, more manageable property. This move allowed them to allocate more funds to travel, a shared passion they had long dreamed of pursuing. They found that the reduced overhead of their new home gave them financial freedom, enabling them to explore new destinations without guilt or stress. Their experience highlights the potential benefits of strategic relocation in retirement, offering a template for others considering similar moves.

Another example is Polina, who found herself balancing family obligations with personal goals after becoming a primary caregiver for her aging mother. This unexpected responsibility required her to adjust her financial plans, prioritizing care costs while maintaining her lifestyle. Polina developed an economic strategy that included support from community resources, ensuring her mother's needs were met without compromising her own financial security. By balancing these competing demands, she could fulfill her caregiving role while continuing to enjoy her retirement. Her story illustrates the importance of flexibility and adaptation in financial planning, showing that it's possible to successfully navigate even the most challenging transitions with careful consideration.

9.3 ALIGNING FINANCIAL DECISIONS WITH LIFESTYLE GOALS

As you enter retirement, it's essential to ensure that your financial decisions are in harmony with your lifestyle aspirations. These choices should reflect the priorities that define your desired retirement experiences. Identifying your core lifestyle aspirations and values is the first step in this alignment. Picture your dream retirement: is it filled with travel, community engagement, or perhaps mastering a new hobby? These aspirations require financial support, so your investments and savings must align with these goals. By focusing on what's most important to you, you can direct your finances to enhance your quality of life, supporting activities that bring joy and fulfillment.

Evaluating financial decisions against lifestyle impacts involves a reflective process. Conducting a lifestyle audit can help you assess whether your current financial choices support your desired lifestyle. This audit examines how your spending and saving habits align with your long-term goals. Ask yourself: Are your investments contributing to the life you want to lead? Prioritize financial decisions that enhance life satisfaction, ensuring your money serves your aspirations. This alignment isn't just about financial security; it's about living a life that resonates with your values. Regularly reassessing your financial strategy allows you to adapt to changes and maintain alignment with your evolving lifestyle goals.

Integrating financial planning with lifestyle aspirations requires strategic thinking. Developing a vision board can be a powerful tool in this process. This illustration of your goals and dreams serves as a steady reminder of what you're working towards. It helps guide your financial planning, ensuring each decision contributes to the bigger picture. Setting lifestyle-focused financial milestones is another effective strategy. These milestones can be specific achievements, such as saving for a dream trip or completing a long-term project. By breaking down your aspirations into achievable steps, you can preserve motivation and track your progress, aligning your financial resources to support these milestones.

Consider the stories of people who have successfully aligned their finances with their lifestyle goals. Take, for example, a couple who prioritized their passion for travel. By carefully planning their finances, they could explore new destinations regularly, enriching their retirement experience. They allocated funds specifically for travel, ensuring that their love for exploration was financially supported. Another individual focused on community service, dedicating time and resources to support local initiatives. By aligning her finances with her values, she found fulfillment and purpose, enriching both her life and the lives of others. These examples illustrate the profound impact of aligning financial decisions with lifestyle goals.

The lessons from these stories emphasize the importance of prioritizing experiences over material purchases. By prioritizing focus, you can create a retirement that resonates with your values. Whether through travel, community engagement, or personal growth, aligning your financial decisions with your lifestyle aspirations leads to a more fulfilling and satisfying retirement. This approach enhances your quality of life and ensures that your monetary resources are directed toward what you value most. By maintaining this alignment, you can enjoy a retirement that reflects your dreams, supported by a financial strategy that serves your goals.

10

ADVANCED FINANCIAL INSTRUMENTS AND STRATEGIES

Envision standing at a crossroads in your retirement planning journey, where each path represents a different financial instrument that can shape your future. Among these paths, exchange-traded funds (ETFs) and mutual funds stand out as robust options, offering distinct advantages for building a balanced portfolio. Grasping these investment vehicles can help you navigate the complexities of financial markets confidently and precisely. Both ETFs and mutual funds are types of pooled investment vehicles, meaning they gather money from multiple investors to enable the purchase of a diversified portfolio of assets. This diversification helps spread risk across various securities, minimizing the effects of poor performance by a single asset on your overall portfolio. The fundamental difference between the two lies in their trading mechanisms and management styles. ETFs are traded on stock exchanges during market hours, much like individual stocks, allowing you to capitalize on intraday price movements. They are typically passively managed, tracking specific market indices, often resulting in lower expense ratios than mutual funds. Mutual funds, conversely, are only permitted to be bought or sold at the end of the trading day at their net asset value. They are usually actively managed, with fund managers making strategic decisions to outperform market indices, which can lead to higher fees.

When selecting ETFs and mutual funds, they should align with your investment objectives and risk tolerance. Start by evaluating the performance and management of the funds you're considering. Look at historical returns to gauge how the fund has performed over time, but remember that past performance does not guarantee future results. Consider the fund's management team and their track record in navigating market conditions. Understanding the objectives and holdings of each fund is equally important. Some funds focus on specific sectors, like technology or healthcare, while others offer broad market exposure. Assess whether the fund's strategy aligns with your financial goals. For instance, a fund focusing on dividend-paying stocks might be suitable if you're looking for steady income. Additionally, keep a close eye on expense ratios, as higher fees can erode your investment returns over time.

Integrating ETFs and mutual funds into your retirement portfolio requires a strategic approach. Combining equity and fixed-income funds can create a balanced portfolio that supports growth and income generation. Equity funds provide exposure to stocks, offering the potential for capital appreciation. In contrast, fixed-income funds invest in bonds, providing stability and regular interest payments. Sector-specific ETFs can target particular areas of the economy, allowing you to capitalize on growth opportunities in industries you're confident about. Consider the example of a retiree who successfully leveraged these instruments to build a diversified portfolio. By allocating a portion of their assets to a mix of domestic and international equity ETFs, as well as bond mutual funds, they achieved a balance that met their risk tolerance and income needs. This approach allowed them to enjoy steady returns while minimizing exposure to market volatility.

Spot Bitcoin ETFs have emerged as a groundbreaking development in the investment landscape, providing a convenient way to track Bitcoin's price without the challenges of directly handling the cryptocurrency. Unlike Bitcoin futures ETFs, which derive their value from contracts based on future Bitcoin prices, spot Bitcoin ETFs are directly linked to the current market price of Bitcoin. This distinction accurately reflects Bitcoin's value, providing investors with a transparent and accessible means of participating in the cryptocurrency market. The introduction of these ETFs has had a notable impact on the market, with increased investor interest and inflows contributing to Bitcoin's price dynamics. Buying into spot Bitcoin ETFs is straightforward, as these funds are available for trading on major stock exchanges., making them accessible through standard brokerage accounts. However, it's essential to be aware of the challenges and risks associated with these investments. Bitcoin's inherent volatility can lead to significant price fluctuations, and regulatory changes may impact the market landscape.

As we look to the future, the landscape of cryptocurrency ETFs continues to evolve, with potential developments on the horizon. Recently, the U.S. SEC approved Ether ETFs, indicating a growing acceptance and classification of Ethereum as a commodity. This milestone opens the door for further innovation in the crypto ETF space, with potential offerings for other digital assets like Solana. As these products become more prevalent, they provide new opportunities for portfolio diversification and participation in the dynamic world of digital currencies.

10.1 REAL ESTATE INVESTMENTS: BEYOND PRIMARY RESIDENCE

Consider the potential of real estate as an investment class that extends beyond the confines of owning a primary residence. A diversified portfolio, including real estate, can provide substantial financial benefits, offering both income generation and asset appreciation. Rental properties, for example, serve as income-generating assets that can supplement your retirement savings. By renting out residential units, you create a steady stream of passive income, which can enhance your financial stability. This revenue can be reinvested to grow your portfolio further or used to cover living expenses, providing a cushion during economic fluctuations.

Additionally, commercial real estate offers another layer of diversification. Investing in office spaces, retail outlets, or industrial properties can yield significant returns and add variety to your portfolio. Commercial properties often come with longer lease terms, providing a more stable revenue stream than residential rentals.

When embarking on real estate investment, it's crucial to have a clear strategy in place. Real Estate Investment Trusts (REITs) offer an affordable entry point for those new to the market. These companies own, operate, or finance income-producing real estate, offering shares to investors. By investing in REITs, you gain real estate exposure without directly managing properties. This approach suits those seeking liquidity, as REITs are traded on major stock exchanges. Those interested in more direct involvement should consider owning properties individually or entering partnerships. Direct ownership allows for complete control over property management and decision-making. On the other hand, partnerships can distribute responsibilities and financial burdens, making it easier to access larger or more diverse properties. Each approach has its merits, and selecting the best depends on your financial goals, risk tolerance, and willingness to engage in property management.

While the prospects of real estate investing are promising, it comes with its share of risks and considerations. Market volatility can create fluctuations in property values, which may affect your investment's profitability. Economic downturns, changes in local markets, or shifts in demand can all impact real estate values. To mitigate these risks, conduct thorough market research and consider diversifying across various kinds of properties and locations. Management and maintenance responsibilities can also pose challenges. Owning rental properties requires ongoing attention to tenant needs, property upkeep, and legal compliance. This can be time-consuming and could require hiring property management services, which add to your costs. Incorporating these responsibilities into your investment plan and budget is essential. Understanding these challenges and anticipating them can help you make informed decisions and maintain the profitability of your real estate investments.

Consider the story of Jana and Silvio, a retired couple who successfully supplemented their income through rental properties. They invested in several residential units in a growing urban area, taking advantage of the steady demand for housing. By attentively selecting properties in desirable communities and maintaining them meticulously, they created a reliable income stream that supported their retirement lifestyle. Their approach allowed them to enjoy financial security while actively managing their investments. Another example is Elton, who diversified his portfolio by investing in commercial real estate. He secured long-term leases with stable tenants by purchasing a small office building. This investment provided consistent returns and appreciated over time, significantly increasing his net worth. These examples highlight the potential of real estate investing to enhance financial well-being, illustrating the importance of strategic planning and informed decision-making.

10.2 BORROWING AGAINST ASSETS: STRATEGIES AND RISKS

Imagine having untapped potential within your existing assets, a financial resource that can be accessed without selling what's already in your possession. Borrowing against your assets can provide this liquidity, allowing you to leverage what you own, such as securities, real estate, or even Bitcoin, to meet your financial needs. Securities-backed lines of credit are a prime example. They let you use your stock portfolio as collateral to secure loans, offering a way to access funds without disrupting your investment strategy. Similarly, home equity loans and reverse mortgages tap into the value of your property. They provide cash that can be used for significant expenses such as home renovations or unexpected medical bills. A reverse mortgage, in particular, allows retirees to receive payments from the equity in their home, offering financial flexibility without immediate repayment. In the digital realm, Bitcoin-backed loans are emerging as a novel option. Using your Bitcoin holdings as collateral allows you to secure loans while retaining ownership of your digital assets, enabling you to benefit from potential future appreciation.

Strategically using asset-backed borrowing can be a powerful financial tool when approached thoughtfully. For instance, funding significant purchases—such as a new car or an unexpected medical expense—without liquidating your investments can preserve your portfolio's growth potential. This approach lets you maintain your investment positions while accessing the necessary liquidity. Managing cash flow can become challenging during retirement transitions, especially as you adjust to a fixed income. Asset-backed loans can help smooth this transition by supplying the necessary funds to cover living expenses or bridge financial gaps. However, weighing the benefits against the risks is crucial to ensure that borrowing aligns with your long-term financial goals.

Despite its advantages, borrowing against assets carries inherent risks that must be carefully managed. One significant risk is the potential for margin calls or losing collateral, particularly with securities-backed loans. Suppose the value of your collateral falls below a certain threshold. In that case, lenders may demand additional funds or liquidate your assets to cover the loan. This scenario can lead to financial strain and impact your long-term security.

Additionally, using property or digital assets as collateral can impact your retirement plans. Over-leveraging can increase debt burdens, reduce your financial flexibility, and erode the value of your assets. Understanding these risks and setting clear borrowing limits can help mitigate potential pitfalls and safeguard your financial well-being.

Consider the story of a retiree who used a home equity loan to cover healthcare costs, allowing them to maintain their quality of life without dipping into their savings. By leveraging their home's value, they accessed funds for necessary medical treatments, illustrating how strategic borrowing can offer a lifeline in times of need. On the other hand, another retiree faced challenges after overextending themselves with multiple asset-backed loans. The burden of repayments strained their finances, highlighting the importance of prudent debt management. These cases provide valuable lessons on balancing the benefits and risks of asset-backed borrowing.

Bitcoin-backed loans present a unique opportunity for those invested in digital currencies. These loans use Bitcoin as collateral, enabling borrowers to access cash while retaining ownership of their Bitcoin. Typically, lenders require a collateral amount more significant than the loan, known as the Loan-to-Value (LTV) ratio, to protect against Bitcoin's volatility. Interest rates and fees can vary, often reflecting the risk associated with the fluctuating value of Bitcoin. Loans can be structured in noncustodial or custodial models, each offering different levels of control and security. Noncustodial models allow you to retain more control over your Bitcoin, while custodial models involve the lender holding the collateral. Repayment terms can include options for early repayment, providing flexibility to manage the loan according to your financial situation. However, margin calls remain risky, as significant drops in Bitcoin's price may require additional collateral or lead to liquidation.

Consider retirees who have successfully used Bitcoin-backed loans. One retiree used Bitcoin to secure a loan for healthcare expenses, preserving their digital assets while accessing necessary funds. Another retiree faced challenges when Bitcoin's value dropped, resulting in a margin call and partial liquidation of their holdings. These examples highlight the importance of understanding the dynamics of Bitcoin-backed loans and managing them prudently. For those looking to maintain financial independence without selling their assets, borrowing against Bitcoin can provide a strategic alternative. This approach mirrors the strategy of property owners who live off their assets without liquidating them, generating tax-free income while preserving their principal.

10.3 INNOVATIVE TOOLS: INTRODUCING THE PERSONALIZED RETIREMENT SCORE

Picture this: you're navigating the complex landscape of retirement planning with a tool that acts like your personal GPS, offering a clear route to your financial destination. This is where the personalized retirement score comes into play, providing an insightful snapshot of your retirement readiness.

To obtain a Personalized Retirement Score, consult a financial advisor or explore online tools offered by reputable financial institutions. Many platforms provide retirement calculators incorporating variables like current savings, expected expenses, income streams, and lifestyle goals. These tools often require personal financial details, such as annual income, projected retirement age, investment growth rates, and anticipated healthcare costs. Some advanced tools use algorithms to provide a more detailed and customized score. Additionally, working with a professional financial planner can offer more in-depth insights, as they can tailor the score calculation to include unique factors, like your risk tolerance and specific retirement aspirations. Whether through digital tools or expert guidance, the key is to ensure that the inputs are accurate and reflect your true financial picture for the most reliable results.

Unlike traditional metrics focusing solely on savings balances or projected income, this score encompasses a comprehensive financial health evaluation. It considers your savings, future income streams, lifestyle goals, and potential healthcare costs. By integrating these elements, the retirement score offers a holistic view of where you stand and what adjustments might be needed to achieve your retirement aspirations.

Using this score involves more than just a number. It's a dynamic tool that helps refine your financial strategies. Begin by identifying areas of strength and weakness within your retirement plan. Perhaps your savings are robust, but your anticipated healthcare expenses have been underestimated. Or maybe your investment portfolio lacks diversification. The score illuminates these facets, allowing you to set precise goals and benchmarks tailored to your unique situation. By focusing on these specific areas, you can make informed decisions to enhance your plan, whether it's adjusting your savings rate, reallocating investments, or exploring new income streams. The retirement score thus becomes a catalyst for proactive financial planning, helping you stay on track and adapt to life's changes with confidence.

The benefits of leveraging a personalized retirement score extend beyond planning. It significantly enhances decision-making and boosts confidence in your retirement strategy. By providing a clear picture of your financial health, the score enables you to engage in more productive discussions with financial advisors, ensuring their guidance aligns with your needs. This clarity demystifies the complexities of retirement planning and empowers you to take control of your financial future. With a clear understanding of your current status and future projections, you can approach retirement with the assurance that you're making well-informed choices. This empowerment is critical to achieving a secure and fulfilling retirement, fostering peace of mind and financial resilience.

Consider the story of Su-Jin, who felt overwhelmed by the myriad of decisions in retirement planning. By utilizing the personalized retirement score, she better understood her financial position and identified gaps in her plan, such as insufficient healthcare savings. With this knowledge, Su-Jin worked with her advisor to adjust her contributions and explore supplemental insurance options, significantly improving her retirement readiness. Her experience highlights the transformative power of the retirement score in optimizing financial plans. Similarly, Sebastian, a retiree who used the score to regularly assess his financial health, made targeted adjustments that allowed him to achieve his goals of traveling and supporting his grandchildren's education. These examples illustrate how data-driven insights can lead to meaningful enhancements in retirement planning.

As you consider integrating the personalized retirement score into your strategy, reflect on how it can provide clarity and direction. This tool is not just about numbers; it's about understanding the bigger picture and making informed adjustments that align with your aspirations. Whether you're just beginning to plan or are well into retirement, the score offers a valuable perspective that can guide your financial decisions. By embracing this innovative approach, you position yourself to navigate the complexities of retirement with greater ease and confidence. This chapter has explored how advanced tools like the personalized retirement score can enhance your financial strategy, setting the stage for our next discussion on continuous adaptation and flexibility in retirement planning.

11

CONTINUOUS ADAPTATION AND FLEXIBILITY

Life's journey is like a winding road, unpredictable yet full of potential. Flexibility becomes your greatest ally as you navigate this path, especially in retirement planning. Life is never static; it throws unexpected changes at us, from joyful events like marriage to challenging ones like health issues. Each shift requires us to reassess our strategies, ensuring our financial plans align with our current realities. The key to thriving in retirement lies not in having a rigid plan but in cultivating the ability to adapt, pivot when needed, and embrace new directions with confidence and clarity.

11.1 ADAPTING TO LIFE CHANGES: FLEXIBLE PLANNING STRATEGIES

Life's milestones—marriage, divorce, becoming a caregiver—significantly impact your financial landscape. Marriage often brings together two sets of economic priorities, necessitating a reevaluation of goals and resources. It's essential to merge plans, ensuring both partners work toward shared objectives while respecting individual aspirations. Conversely, divorce can disrupt financial stability, requiring careful division of assets and a rethinking of retirement timelines. In this case, revisiting your financial plan becomes crucial, allowing you to redefine your path and set new priorities.

Caregiving responsibilities introduce another layer of complexity. Whether caring for aging parents or supporting a spouse with health issues, these roles often demand time, emotional energy, and financial resources. This shift may require reallocating funds to cover medical expenses or adjusting work commitments, affecting income and savings rates. By anticipating these possibilities, you can incorporate flexible strategies, such as diversifying income sources or increasing your emergency fund, to cushion against these demands.

Health changes also dictate financial adjustments. A sudden medical diagnosis or a gradual decline in health can alter your financial needs, prompting a reevaluation of your plans. This might involve adjusting savings rates to accommodate increased healthcare costs or reallocating assets to ensure stability. For instance, transitioning from growth-focused investments to more conservative options can preserve capital and provide liquidity for healthcare needs. Regularly reviewing your plan allows you to make these adjustments proactively, ensuring your financial strategy remains robust and responsive.

Maintaining a flexible mindset is paramount in financial planning. Life is inherently unpredictable, and your ability to adapt is vital. This involves re-evaluating your financial goals annually, considering new developments, and incorporating emerging priorities into your plans. You may have decided to retire earlier than anticipated or pursue a passion project that requires additional funds. By remaining open to revising your plans, you can align your financial strategy with your evolving aspirations, ensuring it supports your vision for the future.

Consider the story of a couple who adjusted their retirement age due to unexpected health issues. Initially planning to retire at 65, they faced a health diagnosis that necessitated an earlier retirement. By revisiting their plan, they adjusted their savings rates and reallocated their investments to ensure financial stability despite the changes. Their proactive approach allowed them to maintain their lifestyle and meet healthcare needs without compromising their long-term goals. This example illustrates the power of flexibility in navigating life's uncertainties and preserving financial security.

Similarly, think of a retiree who altered his investment strategies after downsizing. Having sold his larger home for a smaller one, he used the proceeds to shift his portfolio towards income-generating assets. This adjustment provided a steady cash flow, aligning with his new financial reality and supporting his retirement lifestyle. By embracing change and making strategic adaptations, he was able to enhance his financial resilience and enjoy a fulfilling retirement.

Flexibility in retirement planning is not just a strategy; it's a mindset. It's about preparing for the unexpected, embracing change, and viewing challenges as opportunities for growth. By cultivating this mindset, you equip yourself to navigate life's twists and turns confidently, ensuring your financial plans remain in tune with your goals and aspirations.

11.2 STAYING INFORMED: KEEPING UP WITH FINANCIAL TRENDS

In today's fast-paced world, remaining informed about financial news and trends is vital to making sound retirement decisions. Imagine the financial landscape as a constantly shifting mosaic, where each piece represents a different economic indicator or policy change. Recognizing how these elements fit together can significantly influence your investment strategy. Economic indicators like inflation rates, employment figures, and GDP growth offer insights into the market's health, affecting asset values and investment returns. For instance, rising inflation might erode the purchasing power of your savings, prompting a shift towards investments that offer better protection against inflation. Similarly, understanding how interest rates influence bond prices and stock valuations can guide you in adjusting your portfolio to capitalize on these changes.

Being aware of policy changes that affect retirement accounts is equally crucial. Government decisions on tax laws, Social Security benefits, and retirement account regulations can profoundly impact your savings strategy. A change in tax policy might open new avenues for tax-efficient investing. At the same time, an adjustment in Social Security benefits could affect your income planning. By staying on top of these developments, you can make timely adjustments to your financial plan, ensuring it supports your retirement goals. This proactive approach not only enhances your financial security but empowers you to navigate the complexities of the economic environment with confidence.

To stay informed, it's important to have access to reliable sources of financial information and market insights. Subscribing to financial newsletters and podcasts can provide frequent updates on market trends, economic forecasts, and investment strategies.

These resources, crafted by industry experts, offer valuable perspectives that can aid in decision-making. Additionally, utilizing financial planning software equipped with trend analysis features can provide real-time data and projections, helping you adapt your strategy to current conditions. This blend of human expertise and technological tools creates a comprehensive framework for staying informed, enabling you to make well-rounded decisions in your retirement planning.

Critical evaluation of financial information is a skill that can protect you from misinformation and guide you toward credible insights. Fact-checking sources and cross-referencing data are foundational practices for discerning accuracy in financial news. Engaging with diverse perspectives from reputable analysts and financial publications ensures a balanced understanding of market dynamics. Consulting with financial advisors offers another layer of expertise, providing personalized insights tailored to your unique financial situation. These professionals can help you sift through information, identify opportunities, and mitigate risks, enhancing your overall strategy.

Consider the story of an investor who successfully adapted to financial trends through keen observation and proactive planning. Anticipating an interest rate hike, she adjusted her portfolio by reallocating assets from long-term bonds to equities poised to benefit from the economic shift. This strategic move safeguarded her investments and resulted in significant gains, demonstrating the value of staying informed and responsive to market conditions. Another retiree capitalized on emerging market opportunities by recognizing growth potential in international economies. By reallocating a portion of his portfolio to global equities, he diversified his investments and increased his returns, illustrating how awareness of financial trends can enhance retirement planning.

These examples underscore the importance of remaining informed and adaptable in the face of economic changes. Cultivating a habit of staying updated on financial news and trends will help you make informed decisions that align with your retirement aspirations. Approaching this proactively ensures that your financial strategy remains robust, resilient, and responsive to the ever-evolving market landscape. Through vigilance and informed action, you can master the intricacies of retirement planning with clarity and assurance, securing a future that reflects your goals and values.

11.3 RESILIENCE IN UNCERTAINTY: ADJUSTING PLANS IN VOLATILE TIMES

Financial markets behave as unpredictably as the weather. Economic recessions, like sudden storms, can severely impact your retirement savings. These downturns have a ripple effect, causing stock values to plummet and reducing the returns on your investments. Savings that seemed sufficient can quickly become inadequate, forcing reevaluation and adjustment of your financial strategy. Geopolitical events, such as international conflicts or trade disputes, further complicate the landscape. These events can disrupt market stability, influencing everything from currency values to global supply chains. The interconnectedness of today's world means that even distant conflicts can directly impact your financial well-being.

To maintain stability amidst such uncertainty, building resilience into your financial plans is crucial. One foundational strategy is creating a financial cushion through emergency savings. Having a reserve of three to six months of living expenses can provide a buffer, allowing you to weather short-term disruptions without derailing your long-term goals. This cushion acts as a safety net, preventing the need to liquidate investments during market lows. Diversified investment strategies also play a vital role in mitigating risk. By spreading investments across various asset classes—stocks, bonds, real estate, and commodities—you can reduce exposure to any single market downturn. Diversification ensures that while some assets may decline, others may remain stable or even appreciate, balancing the overall impact on your portfolio.

Adaptability is crucial in navigating volatile times. Being prepared to make timely adjustments to your financial plans is essential. Frequent review and rebalancing of your investment portfolio can help maintain your desired risk profile. As markets fluctuate, your asset allocation may drift from its target. Rebalancing involves selling over-performing assets and buying underperforming ones, restoring your portfolio to its intended balance. This disciplined approach can enhance returns and reduce risk over the long term. Setting predefined triggers for financial plan adjustments is another effective tactic. These triggers could be based on specific market conditions or personal milestones, prompting a reassessment of your strategy when certain thresholds are met.

Consider the example of retirees who have successfully used laddered bond strategies to maintain financial security during stock market downturns. By staggering bond maturities, they ensured a consistent income stream, providing stability regardless of market conditions. This approach allowed them to meet their cash flow needs without selling stocks at a loss. Another example is investors who shifted to defensive sectors during economic slowdowns. By reallocating funds to industries that tend to be less responsive to economic cycles, such as utilities and consumer staples, they preserved capital and reduced volatility in their portfolios. These stories illustrate the power of strategic resilience in maintaining financial security through turbulent times.

Resilience becomes your greatest asset in the face of economic uncertainty. By building a solid financial cushion, diversifying investments, and remaining adaptable, you equip yourself to navigate the challenges of volatile markets. These strategies protect your savings and empower you to seize potential opportunities, ensuring your financial plans remain robust and aligned with your long-term goals. As you continue to adjust and refine your approach, remember that resilience is not just about surviving adversity but thriving despite it.

11.4 EMBRACING INNOVATION: FUTURE-PROOFING YOUR RETIREMENT PLAN

In today's rapidly evolving world, future-proofing your retirement plan involves more than just traditional savings and investments. It means embracing the technological and financial innovations that can significantly enhance financial security. Tech-driven financial tools and platforms have revolutionized how we manage our finances, offering unprecedented control and insight. For instance, financial apps allow you to track your spending, investments, and savings in real time, providing a clear picture of your financial health. These tools can assist you in recognizing trends, establishing goals, and making informed decisions regarding your financial future. Incorporating such innovations into your retirement plan gives you flexibility and precision in managing your resources.

Beyond the realm of conventional investments lies a burgeoning world of new opportunities. Bitcoin, Ethereum, and other digital currencies represent a shift towards decentralized finance, offering potential for diversification and growth. While these assets are volatile, they also hedge against traditional market fluctuations. Exploring these new investment vehicles requires a keen understanding of their mechanisms and risks. Blockchain technology, which underpins digital currencies, offers secure and transparent transactions, decreasing the risk of fraud and enhancing trust in financial dealings. By staying informed and open to these emerging trends, you can diversify your retirement portfolio and increase your returns.

The landscape of financial planning is rich with emerging innovations, each promising to transform how we approach retirement. Artificial intelligence (AI) in investment management is one such trend. AI algorithms analyze expansive data to identify patterns and make predictions, offering more accurate investment insights. This technology can optimize your portfolio, balancing risk and reward with greater precision. Additionally, AI can automate routine financial tasks, freeing up your time for more strategic decision-making. As these technologies evolve, they provide powerful tools for enhancing your retirement strategy, ensuring your plan remains robust and responsive to market changes.

Evaluating and adopting innovative solutions requires careful consideration. The risk-reward balance of new technologies must be thoroughly analyzed before integration into your plan. Assessing the potential benefits and inherent risks is crucial, ensuring that any new addition aligns with your financial goals. Gradual integration is often the wisest approach, allowing you to test the effectiveness of innovations without overcommitting your resources. This methodical process reduces the likelihood of adverse outcomes and positions you to capitalize on successful strategies. By approaching innovation with a critical eye and a willingness to adapt, you can future-proof your retirement plan against unforeseen challenges.

Consider the success stories of those who have leveraged innovation to secure their financial futures. Early adopters of robo-advisors, for example, have achieved significant cost savings and improved portfolio performance. These automated investment platforms offer tailored advice and management, reducing the need for costly human advisors. By embracing this technology, investors have streamlined their financial planning, achieving greater efficiency and accuracy. Similarly, those who have diversified their portfolios with digital assets have reaped the benefits of growth in this nascent market. By strategically incorporating digital currencies into their investments, they have gained exposure to new opportunities while mitigating traditional market risks.

As we conclude this chapter, remember that innovation is not merely a trend but a vital component of a dynamic retirement plan. Integrating technological advances and exploring new investment avenues allows you to position yourself for a secure and prosperous future. This forward-thinking approach ensures that your retirement plan remains adaptable and resilient, ready to meet the challenges of an ever-changing world.

12

LEGACY PLANNING AND LEAVING A LASTING IMPACT

Visualize standing at the helm of a ship, charting a course through uncharted waters, with your legacy as the destination. Legacy planning is akin to mapping this voyage, ensuring that your life's work and values reach those who matter most. At its core, estate planning is about more than just distributing assets; it is about preserving your life's achievements and ensuring they benefit your loved ones. The process begins with establishing a valid will and testament, a legal document articulating your wishes regarding asset distribution. This assures that your estate is managed according to your desires, preventing potential disputes among heirs. Alongside this, creating trusts can provide additional protection and management for your assets. Trusts allow you to set conditions for asset distribution, offering flexibility and control over your estate. They can also bypass probate, ensuring that your heirs receive their inheritance promptly and without the added expense and delays associated with probate court.

Reducing estate taxes and probate costs is a critical aspect of preserving the value of your estate for future generations. One effective strategy is gifting, which involves repositioning assets to reduce the taxable estate. The annual gift exclusion allows you to offer a certain amount to each recipient without incurring federal gift taxes, thereby decreasing the estate's overall value. Life insurance can also play an important role in covering potential estate taxes. Using life insurance to pay these taxes ensures that your beneficiaries receive the estate's total value without the burden of tax liabilities. Such strategies not only maximize the value of your estate but also provide financial security and peace of mind for your beneficiaries.

Selecting the proper estate planning tools is essential to craft a plan that meets your requirements. Trusts, for instance, come in various forms, each with benefits and considerations. Revocable trusts allow you to retain authority over your assets, with the flexibility to alter the trust as circumstances change. On the other hand, irrevocable trusts remove assets from your estate, possibly reducing estate taxes and offering creditor protection. The choice between these trusts depends on your financial goals and personal preferences. Naming beneficiaries and assigning a power of attorney are essential to a well-structured estate plan. Beneficiaries ensure your assets are passed on as intended, while a power of attorney appoints somebody to manage your affairs if you cannot do so.

Consider the story of the Thompsons, a family who successfully navigated the intricacies of estate planning to safeguard their legacy. They utilized a combination of trusts and life insurance to manage their estate, ensuring their children and grandchildren were provided for. By establishing a revocable trust, they maintained control over their assets and avoided probate. Life insurance helped them cover estate taxes, preserving most of their wealth for future generations. Similarly, the Martins, another family, used irrevocable trusts to safeguard their assets from creditors and reduce estate taxes. These examples illustrate how proactive estate planning can effectively manage wealth and protect family interests.

To begin crafting your legacy plan, consider your personal goals and the needs of your beneficiaries. Consider how you want your assets to shape the lives of your loved ones and the legacy you aspire to leave for the future. Remember that estate planning is an evolving process that should adapt to changes in your life and the law. Review and modify your plan regularly to ensure it continues to match your objectives and current circumstances. By taking these steps, you can create a lasting impact that reflects your values and provides for those you cherish.

12.1 CHARITABLE GIVING: ALIGNING FINANCIAL PLANS WITH VALUES

Charitable giving offers a profound way to weave your values into the fabric of your legacy. It allows you to impact the world meaningfully, reflecting what matters most to you and ensuring that your values continue to influence others. Creating a charitable foundation or a donor-advised fund can effectively manage and direct your philanthropic efforts. A charitable foundation can make a structured giving strategy, supporting causes that align with your convictions. This structure can be particularly beneficial if you wish to engage family members in philanthropy, fostering a culture of giving that spans generations. Alternatively, a donor-advised fund provides flexibility and ease, allowing you to make charitable contributions and recommend grants to your chosen organizations over time. Both options enable you to align your philanthropic goals with personal beliefs, ensuring your contributions make a lasting difference.

Tax-efficient strategies are vital in maximizing the impact of your charitable contributions. Contributing appreciated securities, like stocks or mutual funds, can significantly reduce capital gains tax liabilities while offering a charitable deduction for the asset's total market value. This approach benefits the charity and enhances your financial position by reducing taxable income. Qualified charitable distributions from IRAs provide another avenue for tax-efficient giving, particularly for retirees over 70½. Directing required minimum distributions directly to a qualified charity can exclude the amount from your taxable income, potentially lowering your overall tax burden. These strategies allow you to fulfill philanthropic goals while optimizing financial outcomes, making your charitable efforts more effective and impactful.

To develop a comprehensive charitable giving plan, start by setting long-term goals and priorities. Reflect on the causes that resonate with your values, and consider the impact you wish to make. This reflection will guide your giving strategy, ensuring it aligns with your convictions. Evaluating charitable organizations is a crucial step in this process. Research their missions, financial health, and effectiveness in achieving their goals. Tools like Charity Navigator can provide insights into how donations are used, helping you make informed decisions about where to direct your contributions. By prioritizing organizations that align with your values and demonstrate a commitment to transparency and impact, you can ensure your charitable efforts are meaningful and effective.

Consider the story of the Johnson family, who established a scholarship fund to honor their late son's passion for education. By focusing on providing opportunities for underprivileged students, they created a legacy that reflects their values and continues to impact lives positively. The fund has supported hundreds of students in pursuing higher education, embodying the Johnsons' commitment to education and community support. Similarly, the Smiths, a couple dedicated to environmental conservation, used a donor-advised fund to support various green initiatives. Their strategic giving has helped fund projects that restore natural habitats and promote sustainable practices, aligning with their passion for preserving the planet for future generations. These stories illustrate how thoughtful and strategic charitable giving can extend your influence and values beyond your lifetime.

When integrated into your financial and legacy strategies, philanthropy becomes more than just a financial transaction. It transforms into a meaningful expression of who you are and what you stand for. By aligning your charitable giving with your values, you create a legacy that is not only financially sound but also deeply impactful, resonating with future generations and inspiring others to follow your lead.

12.2 PASSING ON WEALTH: STRATEGIES FOR FAMILY AND HEIRS

Wealth transfer planning is pivotal in ensuring that your assets are disseminated smoothly and equitably to your heirs. It is about passing down financial assets, preserving family harmony, and fulfilling your intentions. Setting clear intentions and communicating your wishes to your family is crucial. This involves having open and honest conversations with your heirs about your plans and the reasoning behind them. It helps to prevent misunderstandings and conflicts, allowing your family to appreciate and respect your decisions. Balancing fairness and individual needs can be challenging, especially when dealing with different personalities and expectations. Some family members may require more financial support than others. It is important to consider each individual's circumstances and communicate your reasoning clearly, ensuring everyone understands your intentions and feels valued.

Preparing your heirs to manage and sustain their inheritance is essential when transferring wealth across generations. Family meetings about financial literacy can be a cornerstone in this process. These meetings provide an opportunity to educate family members about financial management, investment strategies, and the responsibilities that come with wealth. It empowers them with the understanding and skills to make educated decisions and manage their inheritance wisely. Establishing family governance structures can also be beneficial. These structures create a framework for making collective decisions and resolving conflicts. They often include family councils or boards that oversee shared assets and promote communication and collaboration among family members, fostering a sense of unity and shared purpose.

Choosing the right tools for wealth transfer is essential to ensuring the process is efficient and effective. Family limited partnerships (FLPs) offer a strategic way to transfer wealth while maintaining control over assets. FLPs allow you to transfer ownership interests to family members, often at a discounted value, reducing estate and gift tax obligations. They also provide a structure for managing family assets collectively, ensuring continuity and control. Lifetime gifting strategies and annual exclusions are also practical tools. Endowing assets during your lifetime can decrease your taxable estate while providing monetary support to your heirs. The annual exclusion lets you gift a particular amount to each recipient without incurring gift taxes, making it a tax-efficient way to transfer wealth.

Consider the example of the Almas family, who successfully passed on their family business to the next generation. They held educational meetings to prepare their children for leadership roles within the company, ensuring a smooth transition and continued success. They preserved the business's legacy by involving their heirs in early decision-making and management. Not only that, but they fostered a sense of ownership and responsibility. In another instance, the Turners effectively used FLPs to transfer real estate holdings to their children. This approach allowed them to maintain control over the properties while benefiting from tax advantages. They established a family governance structure to manage the properties collectively, promoting collaboration and shared decision-making. These examples highlight the importance of transparent planning and communication in avoiding family conflicts and ensuring a seamless transfer of wealth.

By integrating these strategies into your wealth transfer plan, you can create an enduring legacy that preserves your assets, strengthens family bonds, and prepares your heirs for future success.

12.3 CREATING A LASTING IMPACT: BEYOND FINANCIAL LEGACY

Thinking beyond financial assets is essential when considering the legacy you wish to leave. Personal values, ethics, and the life lessons you've accumulated can be just as significant as any monetary inheritance. Documenting personal stories and family history is a powerful way to share these intangible assets. By writing down your experiences and insights, you create a narrative that can guide and inspire future generations. These stories serve as a bridge connecting past to present, offering context and wisdom that mere financial assets cannot convey. An ethical will is another way to express your values and beliefs. Unlike a traditional will, which distributes physical possessions, an ethical will communicates your moral and spiritual legacy. It can include your hopes for your descendants, reflections on your life experiences, and advice for navigating life's challenges. This document becomes a touchstone for your family, a reminder of the principles you hold dear.

Family traditions play a vital role in reinforcing identity and values. Establishing enduring traditions can help solidify these connections, creating a sense of continuity and belonging. Annual family gatherings or retreats provide opportunities to strengthen bonds and share stories. These events can become cherished occasions where family members reconnect, celebrate shared history, and pass down traditions. They offer a platform for discussing family values and fostering unity. Creating family charitable traditions is another way to reinforce collective values. Involving family members in philanthropic activities instills a sense of responsibility and community-mindedness. Whether volunteering together or supporting a chosen cause, these traditions help cement the importance of giving back and acting compassionately.

Mentorship and education are critical components of a legacy that transcends material wealth. By mentoring younger family members, you impart valuable skills and knowledge that can guide them through life's complexities. Setting up mentorship programs within the family allows for structured guidance and support. This can be as simple as discussing career goals, financial planning, or personal development. Encouraging lifelong learning and curiosity further enriches this legacy. By fostering a culture of inquiry and exploration, you inspire future generations to seek knowledge and embrace growth. This approach provides them with practical skills and nurtures an enduring passion for learning.

Consider the account of a community leader who left a profound impact through his values and teachings. His life was a testament to integrity and service. By mentoring young leaders and advocating for education, he inspired countless individuals to pursue meaningful careers and contribute positively to society. Similarly, another individual prioritized values over material wealth, choosing to invest time and energy into community projects and social causes. Her legacy is not measured in dollars but in the lives she touched and the changes she affected. These examples illustrate how a legacy built on values can resonate far beyond one's lifetime, influencing and inspiring future generations.

Creating a legacy that extends beyond financial wealth requires intentionality and reflection. It's about recognizing the impact of your actions and words and how they shape those around you. By documenting your stories, establishing traditions, and mentoring others, you cultivate a legacy that embodies your essence and values. This legacy becomes a guiding light for those who follow, illuminating a path of purpose and meaning. As you consider the legacy you wish to create, consider the values and principles you want to impart. Reflect on your lessons and how they can serve as a compass for future generations. This chapter has explored creating a legacy that transcends material wealth, offering a lasting impact through values, ethics, and teachings.

CONCLUSION

As you reach the final pages of this book, let us take a moment to reflect on the journey we have embarked upon together. As we have explored, retirement planning is not simply about numbers and accounts. It is about crafting a future that aligns with your dreams and values. Throughout these chapters, we have delved into various strategies, from the time-tested reliability of Roth IRAs and 401(k)s to the innovative opportunities presented by Bitcoin and diversified portfolios. Each tool has its place, uniquely contributing to your financial security.

It is crucial to remember the importance of personalized planning. Aligning your strategies with your aspirations and values enhances financial security and enriches your life. This alignment brings a sense of fulfillment and peace, knowing that your financial plan supports what matters most to you. Consider what you want your retirement to look like, who you wish to be with, and what experiences you seek. This vision should guide your financial decisions, transforming them into steps toward the life you envision.

Flexibility and adaptability are your most significant allies in the face of life's uncertainties. As economic landscapes shift and personal circumstances evolve, your ability to adjust your strategies will be key. Be prepared to pivot as needed, explore new financial tools, and adjust your portfolio to reflect challenges and opportunities. This adaptability ensures that your retirement plan remains robust and capable of withstanding life's inevitable changes.

Continuous learning and vigilant research are essential components of successful retirement planning. The financial world is ever-changing, with new developments and trends emerging regularly. By committing to ongoing education, you empower yourself to make informed decisions. This is particularly true in cryptocurrency and Bitcoin, where knowledge is your greatest asset against volatility. Avoid the pitfalls of panic selling by staying informed and viewing market fluctuations as part of a larger, long-term strategy.

Retirement is about more than just monetary security. It is about achieving a balance that allows you to enjoy life fully. Consider the lifestyle aspects—how you will spend your time, engage with your community, and pursue passions that bring joy. These elements are as vital as your financial plans, creating a holistic retirement experience that fulfills your heart and mind.

Remember that a secure and comfortable retirement is within your reach. By applying the strategies discussed, you can confidently navigate the complexities of retirement planning. This confidence stems from knowing you have equipped yourself with the tools and knowledge necessary to face financial uncertainties head-on.

I encourage you to take immediate steps toward refining your retirement plan. Review your current strategies, incorporate the insights gained, and make adjustments where necessary. Each action you take is a step closer to securing your financial future. This proactive mindset will serve you well, enabling you to thrive in your golden years.

Many of the strategies discussed in this book, such as annuities, life insurance, HSAs, long-term care plans, IRAs, 401(k)s, legacy planning, wealth transfer, and charitable contributions, have the potential to integrate with Bitcoin and related technologies in the future. Bitcoin's decentralized and inflation-resistant nature could enhance performance and security by providing an alternative store of value, creating opportunities for tax-efficient growth, and enabling smart contract solutions for automated wealth transfers or charitable giving. As Bitcoin adoption grows, these integrations may redefine how we approach retirement planning, offering innovative ways to safeguard and grow your wealth.

For further exploration, I invite you to engage with additional resources. Numerous books, online courses, podcasts, and financial tools are available to deepen your understanding and support your journey. These resources can provide ongoing guidance, helping you stay informed and adaptable as your retirement approaches.

As we conclude this book, I am grateful to you for permitting me to accompany you on this journey. Your commitment to understanding and preparing for retirement is commendable. I hope the insights have empowered you to take control of your financial destiny. Remember, this is just the beginning. Continue to pursue financial empowerment with curiosity and determination. Your future is bright, and with the right strategies, it promises to be all you have envisioned.

REFERENCES

AARP. (2021). *Understanding long-term care insurance*. Retrieved November 20, 2024, from https://www.aarp.org/caregiving/financial-legal/info-2021/understanding-long-term-care-insurance.html

Above the Canopy. (n.d.). *Retiring with $1mm - A case study*. Retrieved November 20, 2024, from https://www.abovethecanopy.us/case-study-retiring-with-1mm/

Alerus. (n.d.). Beyond Medicare: *How to fund health care costs in retirement*. Retrieved November 20, 2024, from https://www.alerus.com/financial-advice/beyond-medicare-how-to-fund-health-care-costs-in-retirement/

Ameriprise Financial. (n.d.). *Investment strategies for navigating volatile markets*. Retrieved November 20, 2024, from https://www.ameriprise.com/financial-goals-priorities/investing/navigating-market-volatility

Asset Vantage. (n.d.). *Future proofing investment portfolios: The role of technology*. Retrieved November 20, 2024, from https://www.assetvantage.com/future-proofing-investment-portfolios-role-of-technology/

Bankrate. (n.d.). *The 50/30/20 budget rule explained*. Retrieved November 20, 2024, from https://www.bankrate.com/banking/what-is-the-50-30-20-rule/

Berkshire Money Management. (n.d.). *Values based retirement planning: What you need to know*. Retrieved November 20, 2024, from https://berkshiremm.com/values-based-retirement-planning-what-you-need-to-know/#:~

BlackRock. (n.d.). *Five forces shaping retirement*. Retrieved November 20, 2024, from https://www.blackrock.com/us/individual/insights/retirement/five-forces-shaping-retirement

Blue Notary. (2023). *Essential tax and estate planning strategies*. Retrieved November 20, 2024, from https://bluenotary.us/tax-and-estate-planning/

CBS News. (n.d.). *5 smart ways to manage health care costs during retirement*. Retrieved November 20, 2024, from https://www.cbsnews.com/news/smart-ways-to-manage-healthcare-costs-during-retirement/

Charles Schwab. (n.d.). *Bond laddering - Bond strategy*. Retrieved November 20, 2024, from https://www.schwab.com/fixed-income/bond-ladders#:~

Citizens Bank. (n.d.). *Benefits of saving early for retirement*. Retrieved November 20, 2024, from https://www.citizensbank.com/learning/save-early-for-retirement.aspx

Dopp, T. (2021, August). *Cryptocurrency: Insurance industry tests the waters with new initiatives*. AM Best News. Retrieved November 29, 2024, from https://news.ambest.com/articlecontent.aspx?refnum=310901&altsrc145=%7B%7D

Farrington, R. (2021, November 15). *Alternative ways to invest your health savings account (HSA)*. Forbes. Retrieved November 29, 2024, from https://www.forbes.com/sites/robertfarrington/2021/11/15/alternative-ways-to-invest-your-health-savings-account-hsa/

FasterCapital. (n.d.). *Case studies in behavioral finance and investment analysis*. Retrieved November 20, 2024, from https://fastercapital.com/topics/case-studies-in-behavioral-finance-and-investment-analysis.html

Fidelity Charitable. (n.d.). *Charitable contributions: Tax strategies*. Retrieved November 20, 2024, from https://www.fidelitycharitable.org/guidance/charitable-tax-strategies/charitable-contributions.html

Fidelity Investments. (n.d.). *Crypto and estate planning*. Fidelity. Retrieved November 29, 2024, from https://www.fidelity.com/learning-center/wealth-management-insights/crypto-and-estate-planning

Fidelity. (n.d.). *5 ways HSAs can help with your retirement*. Retrieved November 20, 2024, from https://www.fidelity.com/viewpoints/wealth-management/hsas-and-your-retirement

Fidelity. (n.d.). *Guide to diversification*. Retrieved November 20, 2024, from https://www.fidelity.com/viewpoints/investing-ideas/guide-to-diversification

Fidelity. (n.d.). *Tax-savvy withdrawals in retirement*. Retrieved November 20, 2024, from https://www.fidelity.com/viewpoints/retirement/tax-savvy-withdrawals

Fidelity. (n.d.). *Wealth-transfer strategies: Estate tax planning*. Retrieved November 20, 2024, from https://www.fidelity.com/learning-center/wealth-management-insights/tax-efficient-intergenerational-wealth-transfer#:~

Forbes. (2024, January 2). *Bitcoin's role in human rights and global empowerment*. Retrieved November 29, 2024, from https://www.forbes.com/sites/digital-assets/2024/01/02/bitcoins-role-in-human-rights-and-global-empowerment/

Forbes. (2024, October 16). *3 ways Bitcoin is like digital real estate*. Retrieved November 20, 2024, from https://www.forbes.com/sites/edanyago/2024/10/16/3-ways-bitcoin-is-like-digital-real-estate/

FS Blockchain. (n.d.). *Evaluating the impact and future role of Bitcoin Spot ETFs after five months of trading*. Retrieved November 20, 2024, from https://fsblockchain.medium.com/evaluating-the-impact-and-future-role-of-bitcoin-spot-etfs-after-5-months-of-trading-a6b2ee1c8baf

Hallez, E. (2021, April 28). *Bitcoin in annuities? Several insurers are working on it*. InvestmentNews. Retrieved November 29, 2024, from https://www.investmentnews.com/retirement-planning/bitcoin-in-annuities-several-insurers-are-working-on-it/205820

Human Interest. (n.d.). *Different 401(k) employer match types (with examples)*. Retrieved November 20, 2024, from https://humaninterest.com/learn/articles/looking-in-depth-at-the-401k-employer-match/

Investopedia. (n.d.). *Annuities: Pros and cons you should know*. Retrieved November 20,

2024, from https://www.investopedia.com/articles/retirement/08/annuity-mutualfund.asp

Investopedia. (n.d.). *Cognitive vs. emotional investing bias*. Retrieved November 20, 2024, from https://www.investopedia.com/articles/investing/051613/behavioral-bias-cognitive-vs-emotional-bias-investing.asp

Investopedia. (n.d.). *How inflation impacts your retirement income*. Retrieved November 20, 2024, from https://www.investopedia.com/articles/retirement/052616/how-inflation-eats-away-your-retirement.asp#:~

Investopedia. (n.d.). *IRA vs. life insurance for retirement saving*. Retrieved November 20, 2024, from https://www.investopedia.com/articles/personal-finance/100215/life-insurance-vs-ira-retirement-saving.asp

Investopedia. (n.d.). *Mutual fund vs. ETF: What's the difference?* Retrieved November 20, 2024, from https://www.investopedia.com/articles/exchangetradedfunds/08/etf-mutual-fund-difference.asp#:~

Investopedia. (n.d.). *Risks of real estate investment trusts (REITs)*. Retrieved November 20, 2024, from https://www.investopedia.com/articles/investing/031915/what-are-risks-reits.asp

Investopedia. (n.d.). *Roth IRA conversion rules*. Retrieved November 20, 2024, from https://www.investopedia.com/roth-ira-conversion-rules-4770480

Investopedia. (n.d.). *Tax-efficient wealth transfer*. Retrieved November 20, 2024, from https://www.investopedia.com/articles/retirement/07/reduce-estate-tax.asp

Ironwood Financial. (n.d.). *Adapting retirement planning to life changes: A guide*. Retrieved November 20, 2024, from https://ironwoodfinancial.com/adapting-retirement-plans-life-changes-guide/

Medicare Interactive. (n.d.). *The parts of Medicare (A, B, C, D)*. Retrieved November 20, 2024, from https://www.medicareinteractive.org/get-answers/medicare-basics/medicare-coverage-overview/original-medicare#:~

Medicare.gov. (n.d.). *Compare Medigap plan benefits*. Retrieved November 20, 2024, from https://www.medicare.gov/health-drug-plans/medigap/basics/compare-plan-benefits

MicroStrategy. (n.d.). *Key considerations for corporate investment in Bitcoin*. Retrieved November 20, 2024, from https://www.microstrategy.com/bitcoin/documents/key-considerations-for-corporate-investment-in-bitcoin

Money U.S. News. (n.d.). *9 money apps to keep your retirement planning on track*. Retrieved November 20, 2024, from https://money.usnews.com/money/retirement/articles/money-apps-to-keep-your-retirement-planning-on-track

MyUbiquity. (n.d.). *The impact of market volatility on retirement planning*. Retrieved November 20, 2024, from https://www.myubiquity.com/resources/the-impact-of-market-volatility-on-retirement-planning

NAPA-Net. (2024, September). *The critically important and increasing role of retirement plan personalization*. Retrieved November 20, 2024, from https://www.napa-net.org/news/2024/9/the-critically-important-and-increasing-role-of-retire ment-plan-personalization/

National Institutes of Health (NIH). (n.d.). *Lifestyle planning in the transition to retirement.* Retrieved November 20, 2024, from https://pmc.ncbi.nlm.nih.gov/arti cles/PMC11095240/

Next Avenue. (n.d.). *Exploring diverse paths to retirement.* Retrieved November 20, 2024, from https://www.nextavenue.org/exploring-diverse-paths-to-retire ment/

Pension Research Council. (n.d.). *The disruptive impact of FinTech on retirement systems.* Retrieved November 20, 2024, from https://pensionresearchcouncil.wharton. upenn.edu/the-disruptive-impact-of-fintech-on-retirement-systems/

Schwab. (n.d.). *Retirement budget planning: 9 steps to consider.* Retrieved November 20, 2024, from https://www.schwab.com/learn/story/retirement-budget-plan ning-9-steps-to-consider

Schwab. (n.d.). *What is a Roth IRA?* Retrieved November 20, 2024, from https:// www.schwab.com/ira/roth-ira

SmartAsset. (n.d.). *13 retirement planning mistakes to avoid.* Retrieved November 20, 2024, from https://smartasset.com/retirement/retirement-planning-mistakes

SMU Scholar. (n.d.). *Lessons from a case study of secured transactions with blockchain technology.* Retrieved November 20, 2024, from https://scholar.smu.edu/cgi/view content.cgi?article=1281&context=scitech

Sweeney, M. (n.d.). *Case study: How financial planning helped secure their future.* Retrieved November 20, 2024, from https://www.linkedin.com/pulse/case-study-how-financial-planning-helped-secure-mark-sweeney

Thrivent. (n.d.). *Taxes in retirement: A comprehensive guide.* Retrieved November 20, 2024, from https://www.thrivent.com/insights/taxes/taxes-in-retirement-a-comprehensive-guide

True Tamplin, BSc, CEPF®. (2023, July 19). *Bitcoin IRAs: Definition, types, how to set up, benefits & risks.* Finance Strategists. Retrieved November 28, 2024, from https://www.financestrategists.com/wealth-management/cryptocurrency/ bitcoin-iras/

Vanguard Group. (n.d.). *Why invest internationally?* Retrieved November 20, 2024, from https://investor.vanguard.com/investor-resources-education/under standing-investment-types/why-invest-internationally

WebMD. (n.d.). *The emotional shock of retirement.* Retrieved November 20, 2024, from https://www.webmd.com/healthy-aging/features/emotional-shock-retirement

Wise Publishing. (n.d.). *The 5 best robo-advisors for retirees.* Retrieved November 20, 2024, from https://moneywise.com/investing/robo-advisors/best-robo-advi sors-for-retirees

www.ingramcontent.com/pod-product-compliance
Ingram Content Group UK Ltd.
Pitfield, Milton Keynes, MK11 3LW, UK
UKHW020158290926
15471UKWH00005B/948

9 798348 557218